INTERIORS NOW!

INTERIORS NOW!

ED. AURELIA TASCHEN

TASCHEN

CONTENTS

EXPERIENCE
21st CENTURY LIVING

The legendary American decorator Frances Elkins famously liked to keep a firm hold over her clients. She gave them precise charts of the layout of each piece of furniture and every accessory. She only allowed them to display one type of flower – twelve dozen pink and red carnations – and insisted on having the keys to their houses. She would often pop by unannounced and, without asking, make alterations in the event she discovered anything untoward. Recent years have seen a renewed interest in Elkins's style. It's easy to see why. Her signature look – eclecticism, bright colours, pattern-on-pattern, mixing new and old – is very much in synch with today's aesthetic. Her approach, however, is nothing if not anachronistic.

The title of this series – "Interiors Now!" – reads like a manifesto. It comes with the promise of showcasing homes that are timely and of-the-moment. It also poses the question: what exactly is the style of today? Periods in the past are very much linked to distinctive prevailing tastes. The early 20th century was dominated by Art Nouveau and Jugendstil, the 1920s and 1930s by Art Deco, and the 1990s by pared-down minimalism typified by the likes of Christian Liaigre and John Pawson.

In many ways, the first decade of the 21st century saw a reaction to the latter. We have witnessed the return of pattern and wallpaper. We have re-embraced a certain exuberance and rejected the mono-style "total look." Instead, pieces from different periods and vernaculars are combined and juxtaposed. Another trend has been the development of "design as art" – one-off or limited-edition creations produced by galleries that sell for astronomical sums. There has also been a backlash against perfectly "decorated" interiors, where impeccably plumped-up cushions sit on pristine sofas and there's not a hair or a tassel out-of-place. Instead, there's been a move towards rooms with character and quirkiness, spaces that have soul and bear the imprint of their owners – words that would no doubt have Elkins turning in her grave!

This book simply bristles with stellar examples of individualistic interiors. There are those who make their mark with colour, whether it be the all-black Berlin flat of Sylvester Koziolek or the multi-hued Miami home of Doug Meyer. There are collectors, who fill their homes with works of art and objects, about which they are both passionate and well informed. Sometimes the result is stylish and elegant, like Serdar Gülgün's Istanbul apartment, sometimes it's wonderfully provocative like Roland Emmerich's London townhouse. Then, there are others whose personal approach produces something original or completely unexpected. Who, for example, would have imagined one of the hippest designers of today, Marc Newson, to have a traditional, oak-panelled library? He created it for his wife, who has had one in almost every house she has lived, and simply loves the result. As he says, "I thought it was such a wacky thing to do." Check it out on page 292!

WOHNKULTUR IM 21. JAHRHUNDERT

Die legendäre amerikanische Innenarchitektin Frances Elkins war dafür bekannt, dass sie ihre Kunden immer gerne fest im Griff hatte. Sie zeichnete genau auf, wo jedes einzelne Möbelstück und jedes Accessoire platziert werden sollte. Sie erlaubte ihren Klienten nur eine Sorte Blumen - zwölf Dutzend rosa und rote Nelken - und bestand darauf, die Schlüssel zu ihren Häusern zu bekommen. Häufig tauchte sie unangekündigt auf und nahm, ohne zu fragen, Veränderungen vor, wenn sie etwas Unpassendes entdeckte. Seit einigen Jahren ist ein neuerliches Interesse an Elkins' Stil zu beobachten. Diese Entwicklung ist leicht nachvollziehbar, denn ihr charakteristischer Look - Eklektizismus, leuchtende Farben, Mustermix und die Kombination von Alt und Neu - entspricht sehr der heutigen Ästhetik. Aber ihr Ansatz ist höchst anachronistisch.

Der Titel dieser Reihe - „Interiors Now!" - liest sich wie ein Manifest. Er enthält das Versprechen, zeitgemäße und aktuelle Einrichtungen zu präsentieren, und er impliziert die Frage: Was genau ist der Stil von heute? Vergangene Perioden sind sehr stark mit einem vorherrschenden Geschmack verbunden. So dominierte zu Beginn des 20. Jahrhunderts der Jugendstil, die 1920er und 1930er wurden vom Art déco geprägt, und in den 1990ern herrschte ein strenger Minimalismus vor, für den beispielsweise Christian Liaigre und John Pawson stehen.

In vieler Hinsicht erlebte man in der ersten Dekade des 21. Jahrhunderts eine Gegenbewegung zum Minimalismus der 1990er. So kehrten nicht nur Muster und Tapeten zurück, es sind auch eine gewisse neue Überschwänglichkeit und eine Abkehr vom stilistischen „Einheitslook" zu beobachten. Heutzutage werden stattdessen Objekte aus verschiedenen Perioden und Traditionen kombiniert und nebeneinandergestellt. Ein weiterer Trend ist die Entwicklung hin zum „Design als Kunst" - Einzelstücke oder limitierte Auflagen, die von Galerien produziert und für astronomische Summen verkauft werden. Perfekt „eingerichtete" Wohnungen, wo aufgeschüttelte Kissen auf unberührten Sofas sitzen und nicht eine unordentliche Franse oder Troddel zu finden ist, sucht man heute nahezu vergebens. An ihre Stelle sind lebendige Räume mit Charakter getreten, Zimmer, die eine Seele haben und die Handschrift ihrer Bewohner tragen - Worte, die bei Elkins zweifellos Entsetzen hervorrufen würden!

Dieses Buch strotzt vor herausragenden Beispielen individualistischer Interieurs - angefangen mit Innendesigns, die sich durch den Einsatz von Farbe auszeichnen, wie die ganz in Schwarz gehaltene Wohnung von Sylvester Koziolek in Berlin oder das vielfarbig gestaltete Haus von Doug Meyer in Miami. Oder es gibt Sammler, die ihre Häuser mit Kunstwerken und Kunstobjekten füllen, für die sie kenntnisreiche Leidenschaft zeigen. Manchmal ist das Ergebnis stilvoll und elegant, wie etwa die Wohnung von Serdar Gülgün in Istanbul, manchmal herrlich provokativ, wie Roland Emmerichs Londoner Stadthaus. In anderen Fällen bringt ein persönlicher Ansatz etwas sehr Originelles oder völlig Unerwartetes hervor: Wer hätte beispielsweise gedacht, dass Marc Newson, einer der angesagtesten Designer von heute, eine traditionelle Bibliothek mit Eichentäfelung besitzt? Er schuf diesen Raum für seine Frau, die eine solche Bibliothek in fast jedem ihrer bisherigen Wohnhäuser besaß - und sie liebt das Ergebnis. „Ich fand das Ganze herrlich verrückt", sagt sie. Auf Seite 292 können Sie es sich ansehen!

L'ART DE VIVRE AU 21e SIÈCLE

La légendaire décoratrice américaine Frances Elkins était connue pour aimer diriger ses clients d'une main de fer. Elle leur donnait des plans détaillés des pièces, indiquant l'emplacement précis de chaque meuble et objet. Ils n'avaient droit qu'à un seul type de fleur : douze douzaines d'œillets roses et rouges. Elle exigeait d'avoir les clefs de la maison, débarquait souvent à l'improviste et, sans demander l'avis de personne, corrigeait tout ce qui ne lui convenait pas. Ces dernières années ont vu un regain d'intérêt pour son style. On comprend aisément pourquoi. Ses ambiances caractéristiques marquées par l'éclectisme, les couleurs vives, la juxtaposition de motifs, le mélange de l'ancien et du moderne, sont parfaitement en harmonie avec l'esthétique actuelle. En revanche, sa manière de faire serait sans doute moins bien accueillie aujourd'hui.

Le titre de cette collection – «Interiors Now!» – résonne comme un manifeste. Il s'accompagne de la promesse de présenter des demeures contemporaines dans l'air du temps. Il pose également la question : quel est, au juste, le style d'aujourd'hui ? Par le passé, chaque période était étroitement associée à une esthétique dominante. Le début du 20e siècle fut dominé par l'Art nouveau et le Jugendstil, les années vingt et trente par l'Art Déco, les années quatre-vingt-dix par un minimalisme dépouillé illustré par des designers tels que Christian Liaigre ou John Pawson.

A de nombreux égards, la première décennie du 21e siècle a été marquée par une réaction à ce dernier style. Nous avons observé un retour des motifs et du papier peint. Nous avons renoué avec une certaine exubérance et rejeté le total look «monostyle». Nous préférons associer des meubles de différentes époques et les marier à l'artisanat local. Nous avons vu naître le «design en tant qu'art» : des pièces uniques ou en édition limitée produites par des galeries et qui s'arrachent à des prix astronomiques. Nous avons également assisté à une rébellion contre les intérieurs parfaitement «décorés», où des coussins savamment rembourrés sont alignés au cordeau sur des canapés impeccables où pas un gland ni un pompon ne dépasse. Nous leur préférons désormais des pièces qui ont du caractère et une touche d'excentricité, des espaces ayant une âme et qui portent l'empreinte de leurs occupants. Frances Elkins doit se retourner dans sa tombe !

Ce livre déborde de brillants exemples de demeures individualistes. Certains s'expriment par la couleur, l'appartement berlinois tout noir de Sylvester Koziolek et la villa multicolore de Doug Meyer à Miami en sont la preuve. Il y a les collectionneurs, qui s'entourent d'œuvres et d'objets d'art qui les passionnent et sur lesquels ils sont incollables. Parfois, le résultat est chic et élégant, c'est le cas de l'appartement istanbuliote de Serdar Gülgün ; parfois, il est merveilleusement provocant comme l'hôtel particulier londonien de Roland Emmerich. Puis il y a ceux dont la démarche personnelle débouche sur quelque chose d'original et de totalement inattendu. Par exemple, qui aurait imaginé que l'un des designers les plus branchés du moment, Marc Newson, opterait pour une bibliothèque classique toute en boiserie de chêne ? Il l'a créée pour sa femme, qui a toujours vécu dans des maisons qui en abritaient une. Il est enchanté du résultat. Comme il le dit lui-même : «L'idée m'a paru tellement loufoque.» Vous pouvez en juger par vous-même page 292.

ATOTONILCO
GUANAJUATO, MEXICO

OWNER John Houshmand **OCCUPATION** Designer, sculptor and musician
PROPERTY Hilltop villa, 1,115 sqm/12,000 sq ft gross floor; 2 floors; 12 rooms; 6.5 bathrooms
YEAR Building: 2002–05 **ARCHITECTS** David Howell Design, www.davidhowell.net,
Construction liaison: Patsy Dubois, www.patsydubois.com
INTERIOR DESIGNER Steffani Aarons **LANDSCAPE DESIGNER** Luis Franke
PHOTOGRAPHER William Abranowicz, www.williamabranowicz.com

Warm, textural and fun with gorgeous, vibrant Mexican colours used in a minimal way. Finishes were kept sparse to act as a backdrop for the timeless collection of local antiques.
Rustikal und fröhlich, mit sparsam eingesetzten Farben. Die Finishes sind zurückhaltend, damit sie als Hintergrund für die zeitlose Antiquitätensammlung fungieren können.
De superbes couleurs vibrantes mexicaines utilisées avec parcimonie. Les fonds sont dépouillés afin de laisser le devant de la scène à une collection intemporelle d'antiquités locales.

P.12 Situated on nine acres of land outside the quaint artisan town of San Miguel de Allende, this modern-day hacienda has been christened "Tierra Adentro," Inner Land. • Die auf 3,6 Hektar Land außerhalb des Künstlerdorfs San Miguel de Allende gelegene moderne Hacienda wurde „Tierra Adentro", Inneres Land, getauft. • Occupant 3,6 hectares près de la ville coloniale de San Miguel de Allende, un centre d'artisanat, cette hacienda moderne est baptisée « Tierra Adentro » (ou Terre intérieure).

P.13 On the rooftop terrace, Sunbrella acrylic was used to upholster the banquette cushions. • Die Polsterkissen auf der Sitzbank der Dachterrasse wurden

mit Sunbrella-Outdoorstoff bezogen. • Sur le toit-terrasse, les coussins des banquettes ont été tapissés de toiles acryliques Sunbrella.

← David Howell used the architecture to frame views, as here in this inner courtyard. The exterior façades are surfaced with tinted stucco. • Wie hier in diesem Innenhof zu sehen, setzte David Howell die Architektur zur Rahmung von Aussichten ein. Die Außenfassaden sind mit getöntem Putz versehen. • David Howell a intégré des ouvertures dans l'architecture afin d'encadrer des paysages, comme ici dans cette cour intérieure. Les façades ont été enduites d'un stuc teinté.

↑ The house is surrounded by lush and brilliantly coloured landscaping. Grass grows between the stone pavers, mesquite trees sway in the breeze and boulders act as sculptural elements around the pool. • Das Haus ist von einer üppig bepflanzten Gartenanlage in prächtigen Farben umgeben. Zwischen den Steinplatten wächst Gras, Mesquite-Bäume wiegen sich im Wind, und Felsblöcke fungieren als skulpturale Elemente rund um den Pool. • La maison est entourée d'un jardin paysagé luxuriant et coloré. Des graminées poussent entre les dalles en pierre, des prosopis ondoient dans le vent et des rochers forment des sculptures autour de la piscine.

↑ Mesquite stools stand in front of the glazed ceramic kitchen counter. The steel pendant is custom. • Stühle aus Mesquite-Holz vor der gefliesten Küchentheke. Die Hängeleuchte aus Stahl ist maßgefertigt. • Des tabourets en prosopis devant le comptoir de cuisine en céramique émaillée. Le plafonnier en acier a été réalisé sur mesure.

→ In the main dining room, local chairs flank a willow dining table designed by Houshmand. He also created the wrought-iron chandelier in collaboration with Steffani Aarons. • Im großen Esszimmer flankieren lokale Stühle einen Esstisch aus Weide, der von Houshmand designt wurde. In Zusammenarbeit mit Steffani Aarons schuf er auch den guss-

eisernen Kerzenleuchter. • Dans la salle à manger principale, des chaises locales entourent une table créée par Houshmand. Il a également conçu le lustre en fer forgé en collaboration avec Steffani Aarons.

"The interior design was intended to bring in
the flavour and warmth of San Miguel."

„Die Innenausstattung sollte das Flair und
die Wärme von San Miguel widerspiegeln."
« La décoration cherche à faire ressortir tout
le charme et l'ambiance chaleureuse de San Miguel. »

PP. 18–19 A painting by Marion Perlet, a Canadian artist who lives in San Miguel, hangs on one of the rough plaster living room walls. • An einer der grob verputzten Wände des Wohnzimmers hängt ein Gemälde von Marion Perlet, einer kanadischen Künstlerin, die in San Miguel lebt. • Un tableau de Marion Perlet, une artiste canadienne vivant à San Miguel, orne l'un des murs du séjour laissé en plâtre brut.

PP. 20–21 A brick "boveda" ceiling, terracotta floors and a custom concrete tub and wash-basin in the combined master bath and lounge. Vintage sofas flank a John Houshmand maple table. The painting is by Marion Perlet. • Eine „Boveda"-Gewölbedecke aus Ziegelsteinen, Terrakottaböden und eine maßgefertigte Badewanne sowie ein Waschtisch aus Beton in dem Raum, der als Lounge und als Bad dient. An der Wand ein Gemälde von Marion Perlet. • Dans ce salon et salle de bain, un plafond voûté en « boveda », un sol carrelé en terre cuite, une baignoire et des vasques en béton réalisées sur mesure. Deux canapés vin- tage flanquent une table basse en érable de John Houshmand. Le tableau est de Marion Perlet.

→ Traditional Mexican masks hang on the dining room wall. The candleholder was made by a local tinsmith. • Traditionelle mexikanische Masken an der Wand im Esszimmer. Der Kerzenleuchter wurde von einem lokalen Schmied gefertigt. • Masques traditionnels mexicains au mur de la salle à manger. Le chandelier a été réalisé par un ferblantier local.

22

↑ In this guest bathroom, cast-concrete fixtures are offset by the warmth of mesquite wood and a bright wool rug. • Die Betoneinbauten im Gästebad kontrastieren mit dem Waschtisch aus Mesquite-Holz und dem bunten Wollteppich. • Dans cette salle de bain pour amis, l'équipement en béton moulé contraste avec la chaleur du meuble sous-vasque en prosopis et du tapis en laine vivement coloré.

→ A snug nook carved out of volcanic stone is the perfect spot for a siesta. • Die gemütliche, mit Lavasteinen gestaltete Ecke ist der perfekte Ort für eine Siesta. • L'alcôve en pierres volcaniques est idéale pour la sieste.

↑ Local hand-blown glasses and terracotta vases in the sunflower-yellow
kitchen. • Lokale mundgeblasene
Gläser und Terrakottavasen in der son-
nengelben Küche. • Dans la cuisine
jaune tournesol, des vases locaux en
verre soufflé et terre cuite.

→ Vibrant Mexican bed covers in
the children's guest room. • Tages-
decken in kräftigem Grün im Kinder-
gästezimmer. • Dans la chambre d'amis
des enfants, des dessus-de-lit mexicains
aux couleurs vives.

AUCKLAND
NEW ZEALAND

OWNERS Yuri Kinugawa & Owen Hughes **OCCUPATION** Actor & Film producer
PROPERTY House, 120 sqm/1,300 sq ft gross floor; 2 floors; 6 rooms; 1 bathroom
YEAR Building: 2001 **ARCHITECT** Andrew Lister Architect, www.andrewlisterarchitect.com
PHOTOGRAPHER Nathalie Krag/Taverne Agency, www.taverne-agency.com
PHOTO STYLIST Tami Christiansen

The owners wanted something timeless in a modernist style. "Our aesthetic," they say, "is less is more." The layout, meanwhile, was dictated by the Japanese philosophy of "Direct Compass," a branch of feng shui.
Die Eigentümer wollten etwas Zeitloses in einem modernistischen Stil. „Unser ästhetisches Motto", so sagen sie, „lautet ,Weniger ist mehr'". Der Entwurf des Hauses wurde dagegen von der japanischen „Kompassschule" des Feng-Shui bestimmt.
Les propriétaires voulaient un décor intemporel dans un style moderniste. « Notre esthétique, c'est less is more », expliquent-ils. Le plan au sol a été dicté par la philosophie japonaise de « l'école de la boussole », une branche du feng shui.

← The owners were keen to have a double-height living space. Six-metre-high (20 feet) bookshelves were made from black chipboard. White glass globe pendants from the 1950s hang above modern re-editions of Pierre Paulin's famous "Orange Slice" chair.
• Den Eigentümern war sehr an einem Wohnbereich mit doppelter Deckenhöhe gelegen. Die sechs Meter hohen Bücherregale sind aus schwarzen Tischlerplatten gefertigt. Runde Pendelleuchten mit weißem Glasschirm aus den 1950ern hängen über Pierre Paulins berühmten „Orange Slice"-Stühlen, hier in einer modernen Neuauflage.
• Les propriétaires tenaient à avoir une double hauteur sous plafond dans leur séjour. La bibliothèque haute de six mètres est en aggloméré noir. Des globes en verre blanc des années 1950 sont suspendus au-dessus de rééditions modernes du célèbre fauteuil « Orange Slice » de Pierre Paulin.

→ An aluminium ladder on sliding tracks provides access to the bookshelves. • Über eine Aluminiumleiter auf Gleitschienen erreicht man die Bücherregale. • Une échelle en aluminium montée sur rails permet d'accéder aux livres.

P. 28 Perched on a hillside, the entire structure is clad in Canadian cedar weatherboards in order to blend in harmoniously with the surrounding nature. • Das auf einem Hügel gelegene Haus ist vollständig mit kanadischem Zedernholz verschalt und fügt sich harmonisch in die umliegende Natur ein. • Perchée sur une colline, la maison est tapissée de planches en cèdre du Canada afin de se fondre harmonieusement dans la nature.

P. 29 From the deck, the owners enjoy views of Pollen Island nature reserve. In the foreground, the mangroves are at mid-tide. At high tide, they are 95% covered. • Von der Terrasse aus hat man einen wunderbaren Blick auf das Naturschutzgebiet Pollen Island. Die Mangroven sind bei Flut zu 95 % unter Wasser.
• Depuis la terrasse, les propriétaires peuvent voir la réserve naturelle de Pollen Island. Au premier plan, la marée se retire sur la mangrove. A marée haute, 95% de cette dernière est submergée.

↑ Walnut-stained Tasmanian ash-wood units and vintage glass and aluminium pendants in the kitchen. • Im Küchenbereich findet man Einbauteile aus tasmanischer, in Walnussfarbe gebeizter Esche und Vintage-Hängeleuchten aus Glas und Aluminium. • Les éléments de cuisine sont plaqués en frêne de Tasmanie. Au-dessus du comptoir, des plafonniers rétro en verre et aluminium.

→ In the dining area, dark-stained moulded plywood chairs from China are grouped around a contemporary Danish beech table. • Im Essbereich stehen dunkel gebeizte Bugholzstühle aus China um einen modernen dänischen Buchenholztisch. • Dans le coin repas, des chaises chinoises en contreplaqué moulé et teinté entourent une table contemporaine danoise en hêtre.

↑ The walls of the master bedroom are covered in "washi" (traditional Japanese paper) and the floor with tatami mats.
• Die Wände im Hauptschlafzimmer sind mit „Washi", traditionellem japanischen Papier, tapeziert. Auf dem Boden liegen Tatami-Matten. • Les murs de la chambre principale sont recouverts de « washi », un papier traditionnel japonais, et le sol de tatamis.

→ A guest bed on a mezzanine level sports a traditional "tivaevae" quilt purchased from the makers in Rarotonga in the Cook Islands. • Das Gästebett im Zwischengeschoss ziert eine traditionelle „Tiveavae"-Bettdecke, gekauft bei den Herstellern in Rarotonga auf den Cook-Inseln. • Sur la mezzanine, un lit d'amis recouvert d'une courtepointe traditionnelle « tivaevae » achetée chez des artisans de Rarotonga, une des îles Cook.

↑ The Japanese-style bath is made from Lawson's Cypress. The "noren" on the back wall was bought in Tokyo.
• Die Badewanne im japanischen Stil wurde aus Lawsons Scheinzypresse gefertigt. Der „Noren" an der hinteren

Wand stammt aus Tokio. • Une baignoire à la japonaise réalisée en cyprès de Lawson. Le « noren » suspendu devant le mur du fond a été acheté à Tokyo.

→ The small corridor leading to it is draped with "noren" at either end.
• Im kleinen Korridor zum Badebereich hängen weitere „Noren". • Chaque côté du petit couloir qui y conduit est décoré de « noren ».

AUROVILLE
TAMIL NADU, INDIA

OWNERS Jocelyne Blancard **OCCUPATION** Researcher in education
PROPERTY House, 70 sqm/750 sq ft gross floor; 2 floors; 5 rooms; 1 bathroom
YEAR Building: 1984, Remodelling: 2006 **ARCHITECT** Rolf Lieser
PHOTOGRAPHER Toni Meneguzzo/GMAimages, www.tonimeneguzzo.com

The principle was to avoid the rectangular shoebox. Instead, the room shapes are based on the hexagon, and walls are curved rather than linear. Everything is integrated into the structure: tables, shelves, cupboards...
Eine wichtige Bedingung für den Entwurf dieses Hauses war, dass der Bau nicht an eine rechteckige Schuhschachtel erinnern sollte. Räume und Formen basieren auf einem Sechseck, und die Wände sind geschwungen statt geradlinig. Zudem wurde alles in die Konstruktion integriert: Tische, Regale, Schränke ...
Le principe était d'éviter la boîte à chaussures rectangulaire. Les pièces sont hexagonales et les murs courbes plutôt que linéaires. Tout a été intégré dans la structure : tables, étagères, placards...

← The curvaceous windows were made from rods, chicken mesh and glass. • Die geschwungenen Fenster wurden aus Stäben, Kaninchendraht und Glas gefertigt. • Les fenêtres aux formes fluides ont été réalisées avec des tiges, du grillage à poule et du verre.

→ A bed made from mango wood takes centre stage on the loft-like upper level. • Ein Bett aus Mangoholz dominiert das loftartige Obergeschoss. • Un lit en bois de manguier occupe une place centrale dans l'espace à l'étage, laissé ouvert comme un loft.

"The room shapes are based on the hexagon."

„Die Form der Räume basiert auf dem Sechseck."
« La forme des pièces est basée sur l'hexagone. »

P. 38 Four different structures are grouped around the central garden. The fantastical forms of each are made from brick and cement. • Vier verschiedene Baukörper gruppieren sich um den zentralen Garten. Die fantastischen Formen der einzelnen Volumen wurden aus Ziegelsteinen und Zement erschaffen. • Quatre structures différentes ont été regroupées autour d'un jardin central. Elles possèdent des formes extravagantes réalisées en briques et ciment.

P. 39 A view from the front room towards the entrance and flight of stairs. • Blick vom vorderen Zimmer zum Eingang und zur Treppe. • L'entrée et l'escalier vus depuis la pièce située à l'avant de la maison.

PP. 42–43 The kitchen countertop is covered with broken tiles bought loose. The floors are made from terracotta. • Die Arbeitsfläche in der Küche ist mit Fliesenscherben verkleidet, die als lose Ware gekauft wurden. Der Boden ist mit Terrakottafliesen ausgelegt. • Le comptoir de la cuisine est tapissé d'une mosaïque en carreaux cassés. Les sols sont en carreaux de terre cuite.

→ In a work space, a sitar stands on top of a cupboard. In between the doors is an embroidered Tibetan prayer wall hanging. • Ein Sitar auf einem Schrank im Arbeitsbereich. Zwischen den Schranktüren hängt ein bestickter Wandbehang mit tibetischen Gebetssprüchen. • Dans cet espace de travail, un sitar posé sur une armoire. Entre les portes de cette dernière, une petite bannière de prière tibétaine en tissu brodé.

"India is full of colours. What seems daring for Europe is commonplace."

„Indien ist voller Farben. Was für Europa
gewagt erscheint, ist hier alltäglich."
« L'Inde est pleine de couleurs. Ce qui
paraîtrait osé en Europe est ici banal. »

↑ The shape of the open-air bathroom was based on a spiral. Bright colours typical of India were used for each building. According to the owner, they "nurture imagination." • Die Form des offenen Badezimmers basiert auf einer Spirale. Alle Teile des Hauses sind in den für Indien typischen leuchtenden

Farben gehalten. Der Besitzerin zufolge „fördern sie die Vorstellungskraft". • La salle de bain à ciel ouvert a la forme d'une spirale. Chaque bâtiment est peint de couleurs vives typiquement indiennes. Selon la propriétaire, elles « nourrissent l'imagination ».

→ The plastic mirror was bought locally. • Der Plastikspiegel wurde vor Ort erworben. • Le miroir en plastique a été acheté sur place.

AVIGNON
VAUCLUSE, FRANCE

OWNERS Laurence Rigaill & Cyril Jean **OCCUPATION** Sales agent & Graphic designer
PROPERTY House, 220 sqm/2,370 sq ft gross floor; 2 floors; 4 rooms; 2 bathrooms
YEAR Building: 1978, Remodelling: 1999 **ARCHITECTS** Jean-Noël Touche & Christian Chambo
PHOTOGRAPHER Marco Tassinari, www.marcotassinari.com
PHOTO STYLIST Paola Moretti

One of a series of "Bubble Houses" built near Avignon, whose organic curves provide womb-like security. The cave-like interiors are "ideal for a collection of 1960s design, especially oriented towards the Space Age."
Eines der berühmten „Bubble Houses" in der Nähe von Avignon, deren organische Rundungen für eine Geborgenheit wie im Mutterleib sorgen sollen. Die höhlenartigen Räume sind „ideal für eine Sammlung von Designobjekten aus den 1960ern".
Une des « maisons bulles » construites près d'Avignon et dont les formes organiques visent à recréer l'utérus protecteur. Ses intérieurs, évoquant des grottes, sont « idéaux pour accueillir une collection de design des années 1960 particulièrement influencé par l'ère spatiale ».

P. 48 The cement forms of the house were apparently inspired by an imaginary prehistoric creature. • Die Zementformen des Hauses sind offenbar von einem imaginären prähistorischen Wesen inspiriert. • Les formes en ciment de la maison s'inspireraient d'une créature préhistorique imaginaire.

P. 49 A "Panton" chair by the doorway leading into the indoor garden. • Ein „Panton"-Stuhl neben dem Durchgang zum Innengarten. • Un siège « Panton » près de la porte donnant sur le jardin d'hiver.

← Teak stepping stones and a suspended wicker chair in the indoor garden. • Trittsteine aus Teak und ein hängender Korbsessel im Innengarten. • Des marches en teck descendent dans le jardin d'hiver où un fauteuil en rotin est suspendu.

↑ An eye-shaped window provides both a niche for relaxing and a view into the indoor garden. • Das wie ein Auge geformte Fenster bietet sowohl eine Nische zum Entspannen als auch einen Blick in den Innengarten. • Une ouverture en forme d'œil offre à la fois un recoin pour se détendre et une vue sur le jardin d'hiver.

PP. 52–53 The "Bubble Salon" is decorated with a semi-circular banquette and a white cement fireplace. • Der „Bubble Salon" ist mit einer halbkreisförmigen gepolsterten Sitzbank und einem weißen Kamin aus Zement ausgestattet. • Dans le « salon bulle », une banquette en demi-cercle et une cheminée blanche en plâtre.

"Between Barbarella's spaceship, Space: 1999's moonbase and Danger: Diabolik's cavern."

„Eine Mischung aus Barbarellas Raumschiff,
 Mondbasis Alpha 1 und der Höhle aus Danger: Diabolik."
« A mi-chemin entre le vaisseau spatial de Barbarella,
 la base lunaire de Cosmos 1999 et la caverne de Danger : Diabolik ! »

→ Inside, one space flows into the next. The small table to the right is Emma Gismondi Schweinberger's "Giano Vano." • Innen geht ein Raum in den nächsten über. Der kleine Tisch rechts ist das Modell „Giano Vano" von Emma Gismondi Schweinberger. • Les espaces s'enchaînent. Sur la droite, un petit guéridon « Giano Vano » d'Emma Gismondi Schweinberger.

PP. 56-57 In the main living area are two Eero Aarnio chairs dating from 1967. Stools provide seating at the wenge-stained laminate kitchen counter. • Zwei Stühle von Eero Aarnio von 1967 im großen Wohnbereich. An der mit gebeizter Wenge verkleideten Küchentheke kann man auf Hockern Platz nehmen. • Dans le séjour principal, deux fauteuils d'Eero Aarnio datant de 1967. Des tabourets entourent le comptoir de cuisine en stratifié teinté en palissandre d'Afrique.

PP. 58-59 In the guestoom, a concrete platform for a single bed is suspended from the ceiling. The lamp to the right dates from the late 1960s. • Im Gästezimmer wurde eine Betonzwischendecke als Gästebett von der Decke abgehängt. Die Lampe rechts stammt aus den 1960ern. • Dans la chambre d'amis, une plaque en béton en guise de lit est suspendue au plafond. La lampe sur la droite date des années 1960.

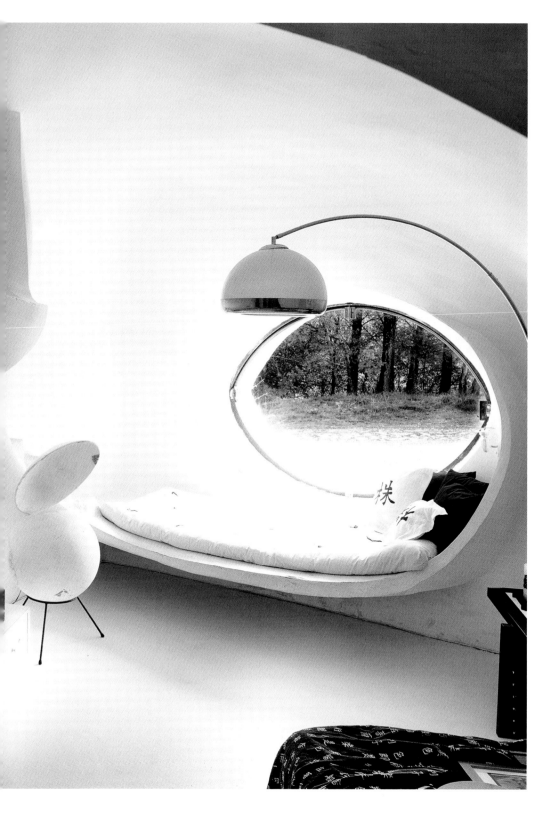

BARCELONA
CATALONIA, SPAIN

OWNERS A Barcelona family **PROPERTY** Villa, 900 sqm/9,700 sq ft gross floor;
1 floor; 11 rooms; 7 bathrooms **YEAR** Building: 1953–63
ARCHITECTS Antonio Bonet Castellana (1913–1989), Antonio Bonet Studio, Buenos Aires
LANDSCAPE Antonio Bonet Castellana & Guillermo, Narberhaus Flamm
PHOTOGRAPHER Verne Photography, www.verne.be
PHOTO STYLIST Ines Daelman, INEZZ Productions, www.inezz.com

The house is characterised by the repetition of a single, vaulted module, sustained by four metal pillars. Attention was paid to its integration into the landscape. The Mediterranean pine trees act as a natural shield.
Kennzeichnend für die Konstruktion dieses Hauses ist die Wiederholung eines gewölbten Moduls, das von vier Metallsäulen getragen wird. Zusätzlich wurde besonderer Wert auf die Integration des Gebäudes in die umgebende Landschaft gelegt. Die mediterranen Pinien wirken wie ein natürlicher Schutzschild.
La maison doit son caractère à la répétition d'un même module voûté soutenu par des colonnes métalliques. Un grand soin a été porté à son intégration dans le paysage. Aujourd'hui, les pins méditerranéens forment un écran naturel protecteur.

P. 60 Flanked by a large lawn and swimming pool, the one-storey villa offers stunning views of the Mediterranean Sea. • Flankiert von einer großen Rasenfläche und einem Swimmingpool, bietet die eingeschossige Villa einen fantastischen Blick auf das Mittelmeer. • Prolongée par une vaste pelouse et une piscine, la villa de plain-pied jouit de superbes vues sur la Méditerranée.

P. 61 A view of one of the structural modules which make up the villa. The table and chairs in the garden are made from stone. • Ansicht eines Baumoduls, das das Grundelement der Villenkonstruktion bildet. Der Tisch und die Stühle im Garten sind aus Stein gefertigt. • Un des modules structurels qui composent la villa. La table et les sièges du jardin sont en pierre.

PP. 62-63 The glass-walled entrance hall looking into the huge living room. • Die verglaste Eingangshalle mit Blick ins ausschweifende Wohnzimmer. • L'entrée vitrée donnant sur le séjour exubérant.

← Wooden blinds were installed to filter the lightin the living room. • Holzläden filtern den Lichteinfall im Wohnzimmer. • Des stores en bois filtrent la lumière du séjour.

↑ The tan leather sofa was designed by the architect of the villa. • Das braune Ledersofa wurde von dem Architekten der Villa entworfen. • Le canapé en cuir caramel a été dessiné par l'architecte de la villa.

PP. 66-67 The owner requested a living room big enough to host private concerts. • Auf Wunsch des Eigentümers sollte das Wohnzimmer groß genug sein, um private Konzerte darin veranstalten zu können. • Le propriétaire tenait à ce que le séjour soit assez spacieux pour accueillir des concerts privés.

↑ A storage cupboard divides the main dining room from this informal eating area. • Ein Schrank dient als Trennwand zwischen dem großen Esszimmer und einem Essbereich. • Un meuble de rangement sert de cloison entre la salle à manger et ce coin repas.

→ A cupboard is faced with a photo of a local plant. • Der Hängeschrank wurde mit der Fotografie einer einheimischen Pflanze verkleidet. • Une armoire tapissée de la photo d'une plante locale.

P. 70–71 Hans Wegner chairs in front of a desk in the master bedroom. • Stühle von Hans Wegner im Hauptschlafzimmer. • Dans la chambre principale, des chaises de Hans Wegner devant un long bureau.

↑ → Plants adorn the interior; multi-coloured glass is a recurrent element in the villa. • Die Pflanzen im Haus wurden in das Interieur integriert. Das mehrfarbige Glasmotiv ist ein wiederkehrendes Element der Villa. • Des plantes poussent à l'intérieur de la villa ; les motifs en verre multicolore forment un thème récurrent.

BARCELONA
CATALONIA, SPAIN

OWNERS Benedetta Tagliabue **OCCUPATION** Architect **PROPERTY** House
600 sqm/6,500 sq ft gross floor; 2 floors; 5 rooms; 3 bathrooms
YEAR Building: 18th century, Remodelling: 1993–94 **ARCHITECT &**
INTERIOR DESIGNER Miralles Tagliabue EMBT, www.mirallestagliabue.com
PHOTOGRAPHER Conrad White/Zapaimages

A highly unconventional apartment at the heart of Barcelona's Gothic quarter. The breathtaking main living room was kept as open as possible. "It was," says owner Benedetta Tagliabue, "like finding a loft in a historic building."
Eine unkonventionelle Wohnung im gotischen Viertel von Barcelona. Das Hauptwohnzimmer wurde so offen wie möglich gehalten. „Es war", so die Besitzerin Benedetta Tagliabue, „als würde man mitten in einem historischen Gebäude ein Loft entdecken."
Un appartement très original au cœur du quartier gothique de Barcelone. Le grand salon a été conservé le plus ouvert possible. Benedetta Tagliabue, la propriétaire, explique : « C'était comme découvrir un loft dans un bâtiment historique. »

"Learning to live with a given structure, like rummaging through the pockets of an old coat."

„Mit einem vorgegebenen Bauwerk leben zu lernen ist, wie in den Taschen eines alten Mantels herumzukramen."

« Apprendre à vivre dans une structure ancienne, c'est un peu comme de fouiller dans les poches d'un vieux manteau. »

P. 74 The spacious apartment wraps itself around a central courtyard in one of the oldest parts of Barcelona. • Die geräumige Wohnung erstreckt sich rund um einen zentralen Innenhof in einem der ältesten Viertel Barcelonas. • L'appartement spacieux s'enroule autour d'une cour centrale dans l'un des plus vieux quartiers de Barcelone.

P. 75 A rather grand flight of steps provides access to the "piano nobile." • Eine imposante Treppe führt hinauf in die Beletage. • Un bel escalier en pierre mène au « piano nobile ».

→ Bookshelves were installed and the ceiling left open. • Bücherregale wurden aufgestellt und die Decke geöffnet. • Des bibliothèques ont été installées tout autour de la pièce et le plafond a été laissé ouvert sur l'étage supérieur.

PP. 78-79 A table designed by Enric Miralles dominates the entrance hall. The vase was found buried in the courtyard. The "Butterfly" chair is by Antonio Bonet Castellana. • Ein von Enric Miralles designter Tisch beherrscht die Eingangshalle. Die Vase fand sich im Innenhof; der „Butterfly"-Sessel ist ein Entwurf von Antonio Bonet Castellana. • Le hall d'entrée est dominé par une table dessinée par Enric Miralles. Le vase a été déterré dans la cour. Fauteuil « Papillon » d'Antonio Bonet Castellana.

← The old paintings in Benedetta Tagliabue's study are in an incredible state of preservation because they were covered with wallpaper for several hundred years. • Die alten Wandmalereien im Arbeitszimmer von Benedetta Tagliabue sind deshalb so gut erhalten, weil sie mehrere Hundert Jahre mit Tapeten bedeckt waren. • Ayant été recouvertes de papier peint pendant des siècles, les fresques anciennes dans le bureau de Benedetta Tagliabue sont dans un excellent état de conservation.

↑ An old Indian bed stands in front of a frescoed wall. • Ein altes indisches Bett vor einer Wand mit Fresken. • Un vieux lit indien devant un mur couvert d'une fresque.

↑ Tagliabue found the porcelain lamp on the piano in Windsor. • Die Porzellanlampe auf dem Klavier entdeckte Tagliabue in Windsor. • Tagliabue a déniché à Windsor la lampe en porcelaine sur le piano.

→ In the main living room, antique tiles were inserted like rugs into the wooden parquet. The old north Italian stove was a present from Tagliabue's father and now acts as a cupboard. The "Lounge Chair" is a classic by Charles and Ray Eames. • Im Hauptwohnzimmer sind antike Kacheln wie Teppiche in das Holzparkett eingefügt. Der alte norditalienische Ofen ist ein Geschenk von Tagliabues Vater und fungiert jetzt als Schrank. Der „Lounge Chair" ist ein Klassiker von Charles und Ray Eames. • Dans le grand séjour, des carreaux anciens ont été insérés dans le plancher comme des tapis. Le vieux poêle provenant d'Italie du Nord est un cadeau du père de Tagliabue et a été converti en armoire. Le fauteuil « Lounge » est un classique de Charles et Ray Eames.

← The iroko wood furniture in the kitchen was designed by Tagliabue and Miralles. • Die Küchenmöbel aus Iroko-Holz entstanden nach Entwürfen von Tagliabue und Miralles. • Les meubles de cuisine en bois d'iroko ont été conçus par Tagliabue et Miralles.

↑ An Eames rocking chair and a light fixture from the late 1950s in a salon used for reading and watching TV. • Ein Eames-Schaukelstuhl und eine Lampe aus den späten 1950ern in einem kleinen Salon • Dans un petit salon, un rocking-chair de Charles et Ray Eames et un plafonnier de la fin des années 1950.

PP. 86–87 The wall paintings in the master bedroom were discovered during the renovation. • Die Wandbilder im Hauptschlafzimmer wurden bei der Renovierung entdeckt. • Les fresques dans la chambre principale ont été découvertes lors des travaux de rénovation.

BEIJING
CHAOYANG DISTRICT, CHINA

OWNERS Kelly Li Hong Yu **OCCUPATION** Interior designer
PROPERTY Duplex, 500 sqm/5,400 sq ft gross floor;
2 floors; 4 rooms; 4 bathrooms **YEAR** Building: 2000, Remodelling: 2002
INTERIOR DESIGNERS Mo Ping, Simon Wu (Full Interior Designer)
PHOTOGRAPHER Reto Guntli/TASCHEN, www.retoguntli.com

The owner was attracted by the light in this duplex in a highrise. Her goal was to create a "contemporary international style in China": free-flowing, open spaces and a savvy mix of Western design and Chinese antiques.
Die Besitzerin war von dem Licht in dieser Wohnung in einem Hochhaus begeistert. Sie wollte fließende, offene Räume mit einer intelligenten Mischung aus westlichem Design und chinesischen Antiquitäten.
La propriétaire fut séduite par la lumière de ce duplex d'un gratte-ciel moderne. Son but : créer « un style international contemporain en Chine », qui se traduit par des espaces ouverts et fluides accueillant un savant mélange de mobilier design occidental et d'antiquités chinoises.

P. 88 Sweeping views of the towers of the Chaoyang District to the east of central Beijing. Rem Koolhaas's CCTV tower is not far away. • Ein beeindruckender Blick auf die Türme des Bezirks Chaoyang im Osten des Zentrums von Peking. Der CCTV Tower von Rem Koolhaas befindet sich ganz in der Nähe. • Des vues panoramiques sur les tours du quartier Chaoyang à l'est du centre de Pékin. La tour de la CCTV conçue par Rem Koolhaas se dresse non loin.

P. 89 The Qing Dynasty chair on the upstairs landing was carved from huanghuali wood. • Der Stuhl aus der Qing-Dynastie auf dem oberen Treppenabsatz ist aus Huanghuali-Holz geschnitzt. • Sur le palier, un fauteuil en huanghuali sculpté datant de la dynastie Qing.

↓ A Thai Buddha stands on the island in the kitchen. The ceiling light was designed by Mo Ping. • Ein thailändischer Buddha auf der Kochinsel in der Küche. Die Deckenleuchte wurde von Mo Ping designt. • Bouddha thaïlandais sur l'îlot de cuisine. Lustre conçu par Mo Ping.

↑ A small seating area, which Hong Yu sometimes uses for reading a paper. The red bowl was originally intended for fish. • Eine kleine Sitzecke, die Hong Yu gelegentlich zum Zeitunglesen nutzt. Das große rote Gefäß war ursprünglich für Fische bestimmt. • Un petit coin salon où Hong Yu aime parfois s'asseoir pour lire son journal. La vasque rouge était initialement conçue pour accueillir des poissons.

PP. 92–93 The folding Qing Dynasty screen once belonged to Li Lian Ying, the head eunuch at the Imperial Court, who made a fortune from bribery. • Der Wandschirm aus der Qing-Dynastie gehörte einst Li Lian Ying, dem berüchtigten Eunuchen am Kaiserhof, der mit Bestechungsgeldern ein Vermögen machte. • Le paravent datant de la dynastie Qing appartenait autrefois à Li Lian Ying, le chef eunuque de la cour impériale, célèbre pour avoir fait fortune grâce à la corruption.

← East meets West in the study. The rug is from Tibet and the chairs from Italy. • East meets West im Arbeitszimmer: Der Teppich kommt aus Tibet, die Stühle sind aus Italien. • Dans le bureau, la rencontre de l'Occident et de l'Orient. Le tapis est tibétain et les chaises sont italiennes.

↑ In the conservatory space on the upper floor, two "Café" armchairs

designed by Piero Lissoni for Living Divani are placed in front of antique Chinese vases. • Im Wintergarten im oberen Stock stehen zwei „Café"-Sessel von Piero Lissoni, die er für Living Divani entworfen hat, vor antiken chinesischen Vasen. • Dans le petit jardin d'hiver à l'étage supérieur, deux fauteuils « Café » dessinés par Piero Lissoni pour Living Divani devant une collection de vases chinois anciens.

PP. 96–97 White marble was used in the master bathroom. The sink is from Flaminia. • Im Bad wurde weißer Marmor verwendet. Das Waschbecken ist von Flaminia. • Dans la salle de bain principale, le marbre blanc domine. Le lavabo vient de chez Flaminia.

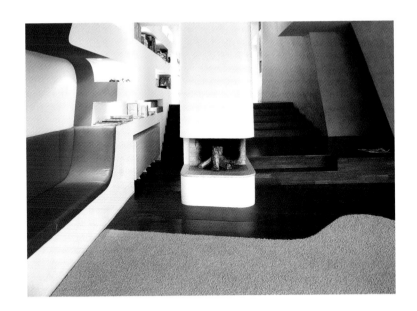

BERLIN
PRENZLAUER BERG, GERMANY

OWNERS Dirk Fabarius **OCCUPATION** Media Entrepeneur
PROPERTY Apartment, 350 sqm/3,800 sq ft gross floor; 1 floor;
1-6 rooms; 3 bathrooms **YEAR** Building: 19th century, Remodelling: 2003-04
ARCHITECT & INTERIOR DESIGNER GRAFT, www.graftlab.com
PHOTOGRAPHER Ludger Paffrath, www.ludger-paffrath.de

The flat was opened up and beds, benches, sofas, walk-in closets and shelves integrated into a curvaceous, dry wall construction. This one continuous space can be subdivided into six thanks to concealed partitions.

Die Wohnung wurde geöffnet und Betten, Bänke, Sofas, begehbare Kleiderschränke sowie Regale in eine geschwungene, alles umschließende Trockenwand-Konstruktion integriert. Dieser große Raum kann durch Abtrennungen in sechs kleinere Räume unterteilt werden.

Les cloisons ont été abattues et les lits, bancs, canapés, penderies et étagères intégrés dans une structure en plâtre qui s'enroule autour du grand espace ouvert. Grâce à des cloisons cachées, celui-ci peut se diviser en six espaces plus petits.

P. 98 One of the owner's prerequisites for the apartment was a fireplace, seen here in the living room. The flat measures almost 35 metres (115 feet from one side to the other). • Eine der Vorgaben des Besitzers beim Entwurf des Apartments war ein Kamin, der hier im Wohnzimmer zu sehen ist. Von einem Ende zum anderen misst die Wohnung fast 35 Meter. • Le propriétaire tenait à avoir une cheminée, que l'on voit ici dans la partie séjour. L'appartement mesure près de 35 mètres d'un bout à l'autre.

P. 99 Niches with banquette seating are integrated into the curving dry wall structure, which runs around the perimeter of the space. • In die geschwungene Trockenwand-Konstruktion, die die gesamte Wohnung umschließt, wurden Nischen mit Sitzbänken integriert. • Des niches équipées de banquettes ont été intégrées dans la structure en courbes qui borde tout le périmètre de l'espace ouvert.

↑ → The smoked oak stairs lead up to the roof terrace; a set of Pierre Paulin "Little Tulip" chairs are grouped around the American walnut dining table. • Die Treppe aus dunkel gebeizter Eiche führt hinauf zur Dachterrasse. „Little Tulip"-Stühle von Pierre Paulin rund um einen Esstisch aus amerikanischem Nussbaum. • Les marches tapissées de lattes en chêne fumé mènent à la terrasse sur le toit ; une série de chaises « Little Tulip » de Pierre Paulin entourent la table américaine en noyer.

↑ A view from the master bedroom with its smoked oak parquet flooring into the bathroom. • Blick vom Hauptschlafzimmer mit seinem Parkett aus dunkel gebeizter Eiche ins Badezimmer. • La chambre principale avec son parquet en chêne fumé qui s'étend jusque dans la salle de bain.

→ Keith Haring's lithograph entitled "Dog" hangs above the fireplace. • Über dem Kamin hängt Keith Harings Lithografie „Dog". • Au-dessus de la cheminée, une lithographie de Keith Haring, « Dog ».

← The bed is integrated into yet another built-in element. A mustard-coloured paper was chosen for the walls. • Das Bett ist in ein weiteres Einbauelement integriert. Für die Wände wurde eine senffarbene Tapete gewählt. • Le lit est lui aussi encastré dans la structure. Le mur est tapissé d'un papier peint jaune moutarde.

↑ A hole in the wall in the guest bathroom provides a sneak view of the adjacent living room. • Durch eine Öffnung in der Wand des Gästebads kann man einen Blick in das angrenzende Wohnzimmer werfen. • Dans la salle de bain des invités, une ouverture permet d'observer ce qui se passe dans le séjour adjacent.

BERLIN

MITTE, GERMANY

OWNER Sylvester Koziolek **OCCUPATION** Interior and set designer
PROPERTY Apartment, 115 sqm/1,240 sq ft gross floor; 1 floor; 2 rooms;
1 bathroom **YEAR** Building: early 20th century, Remodelling: 1996
INTERIOR DESIGNER Sylvester Koziolek, www.sylvesterk.tumblr.com
PHOTOGRAPHER Ludger Paffrath, www.ludger-paffrath.de **PHOTO PRODUCER** Andreas Tölke

An apartment in which almost everything is black – the walls, the ceiling, the floors. For the owner Sylvester Koziolek, the colour sets the perfect stage for his stellar collection of 20th-century design pieces.
In dieser Wohnung ist fast alles schwarz – die Wände, die Decken, die Böden. Für Eigentümer Sylvester Koziolek bildet diese Farbe den perfekten Hintergrund für seine herausragende Sammlung von Designobjekten des 20. Jahrhunderts.
Un appartement où presque tout est noir : les murs, le plafond, les sols. Pour le propriétaire, Sylvester Koziolek, c'est le décor idéal pour mettre en valeur sa superbe collection de pièces design du 20e siècle.

P. 106 Owner Sylvester Koziolek is pictured in an Osvaldo Borsani armchair in the living room. • Eigentümer Sylvester Koziolek in einem Sessel von Osvaldo Borsani im Wohnzimmer. • Dans le séjour, le propriétaire Sylvester Koziolek assis dans un fauteuil d'Osvaldo Borsani.

P. 107 A view from the hallway towards the living room. The table in the foreground is by Carl Auböck and the chair on the left was designed by Franco Albini in 1955. • Blick aus der Diele ins Wohnzimmer. Der Tisch im Vordergrund

stammt von Carl Auböck, der Stuhl links wurde 1955 von Franco Albini entworfen. • Vue du séjour depuis le hall d'entrée. Au premier plan, une table basse de Carl Auböck. Le fauteuil à gauche a été dessiné par Franco Albini en 1955.

↑ A selection of ceramics and toys on a Mario Bellini console. • Eine Auswahl von Keramiken und Spielzeug auf einer Konsole von Mario Bellini. • Un ensemble de céramiques et de jouets sur une console de Mario Bellini.

→ To the right, a Gaetano Pesce bowl stands on a Hans Bellmann table. In the display cabinet are Bauhaus ceramics that Koziolek has collected over the years. • Rechts auf dem Tisch von Hans Bellmann steht eine Schale von Gaetano Pesce. In dem Vitrinenschrank ist eine Sammlung von Bauhaus-Keramiken zu sehen, die Koziolek über die Jahre zusammengetragen hat. • A droite, une coupe de Gaetano Pesce sur une table de Hans Bellman. Le meuble vitrine abrite une collection de céramiques Bauhaus constituée par Koziolek au fil des ans.

"I never found black surroundings
to be particularly unusual."

„Eine schwarze Umgebung war für mich
nie besonders ungewöhnlich."
« Je ne vois pas ce qu'un environnement
noir a d'insolite. »

← The red tiles in the kitchen are one of
the rare exceptions to the all-black rule.
A pair of 1950s sconces shine light onto
a coffee and tea service created by the
German ceramicist, Hedwig Bollhagen.
• Die roten Kacheln in der Küche stellen
eine der seltenen Ausnahmen zum
dominierenden Schwarz dar. Ein Paar
Wandlampen aus den 1950ern beleuch-
ten ein Kaffee- und Teeservice der deut-
schen Keramikerin Hedwig Bollhagen.
• Les carreaux rouges de la cuisine sont
l'une des rares exceptions à la règle du
« tout noir ». Une paire d'appliques des
années 1950 illumine un service à café
et à thé créé par la céramiste allemande
Hedwig Bollhagen.

↑ A Venini light fixture hangs in the bathroom. • Eine Venini-Leuchte im Badezimmer. • Un plafonnier Venini est suspendu dans la salle de bain.

→ In the bedroom, an Arne Jacobsen "AJ" lamp stands on a George Nelson table. The goatskin headboard was designed by Koziolek and is almost 2.5 metres (8.2 feet) high. • Eine „AJ"-Lampe von Arne Jacobsen auf einem Tisch von George Nelson im Schlafzimmer. Das fast 2,5 Meter hohe Kopfteil aus Ziegenleder wurde von Koziolek selbst entworfen. • Dans la chambre, une lampe « AJ » d'Arne Jacobsen posée sur un guéridon de George Nelson. Koziolek a conçu lui-même la tête de lit en peau de chèvre qui mesure près de 2,5 mètres de haut.

BERLIN
PRENZLAUER BERG, GERMANY

OWNER Luzia Braun **OCCUPATION** TV presenter and journalist
PROPERTY Apartment, 150 sqm/1,600 sq ft gross floor; 1 floor;
2 levels; 3 rooms; 2 bathrooms **YEAR** Remodelling: 2007
ARCHITECT & INTERIOR DESIGNER Thomas Bendel, www.thomasbendel.de
PHOTOGRAPHER Hiepler & Brunier, www.hiepler-brunier.de **PHOTO STYLIST** Thomas Rook

Rectilinear lines, simple forms and a lack of architectural detailing create a contemporary framework for each of the very open spaces. Functionality is provided by barely perceptible storage units throughout.
Klare Linien, schlichte Formen und sparsame architektonische Details sorgen in jedem der sehr offenen Räume für einen modernen Rahmen. Funktionalität wird durch die kaum sichtbaren integrierten Schränke gewährleistet.
Des lignes droites, des formes simples et l'absence de détails architecturaux créent un cadre contemporain dans chacun des espaces ouverts. Des meubles de rangement habilement dissimulés assurent la fonctionnalité.

P. 114 A view towards the living room from the office, which doubles as a guest bedroom. The vintage tubular furniture in the background is by Thonet. • Blick vom kombinierten Arbeits- und Gäste-zimmer zum Wohnzimmer. Die Stahl-rohrmöbel im Hintergrund sind Klassiker von Thonet. • Vue du séjour depuis le bureau / chambre d'amis. Le classeur à rideau ancien sur la droite est un Thonet.

P. 115 The 1960s Venini lights above the table are made from Murano glass. A grey oiled oak veneer was used for the bookcases. • Die Venini-Leuchten aus den 1960ern über dem Tisch sind aus Muranoglas gefertigt. Für die Bücher-regale wurde ein grau gebeiztes und geöltes Eichenfurnier verwendet. • Les plafonniers Venini des années 1960 sont en verre de Murano. Les cloisons

de la bibliothèque sont tapissées d'un placage en chêne passé à la cire grise.

← An old bentwood Thonet chair and glass salt and pepper shakers from Holmegaard. • Ein alter Bugholzstuhl von Thonet und gläserne Salz- und Pfefferstreuer von Holmegaard. • Une chaise Thonet ancienne en bois courbé et une salière et poivrière en verre de chez Holmegaard.

↑ The solid oak dining table was designed by Thomas Bendel. Elements from a 1960s Poggenpohl kitchen were integrated into the new design. • Der Esstisch aus massiver Eiche wurde von Thomas Bendel entworfen. Elemente einer Poggenpohl-Küche aus den 1960ern sind in das neue Design inte-griert. • La table en chêne de la salle

à manger à été dessinée par Thomas Bendel. La cuisine moderne intègre des éléments d'une cuisine Poggenpohl des années 1960.

P. 118–119 An oak-clad unit integrates a number of functions. The stairs lead to the roof terrace and the double bed offers a stunning view of the TV tower on Alexanderplatz. • Das mit Eichenholz verkleidete Element vereinigt eine Reihe von Funktionen. Die Treppe führt zur Dachterrasse, und von der Liegeebene aus bietet sich ein fantastischer Blick zum Fernsehturm auf dem Alexanderplatz. • Module plaqué en chêne multifonctions. L'escalier mène à la terrasse sur le toit. Du grand lit, on a une vue superbe sur la tour de télé d'Alexanderplatz.

PP. 120–121 The living and dining areas are separated by a double-sided fireplace. • Wohn- und Essbereich sind durch einen nach beiden Seiten offenen Kamin getrennt. • Le séjour et la salle à manger sont séparés par une cheminée à double foyer.

↑ An opaque glass door leads into the shower. • Durch eine Tür aus Opakglas gelangt man in die Dusche. • Une porte en verre opaque s'ouvre sur la douche.

→ The corridor connects the bedroom to the kitchen and dining room at the top of the steps. • Vom Schlafzimmer gelangt man über eine Treppe im Arbeitsbereich zu Küche und Esszimmer. • Le couloir relie la chambre à la cuisine et à la salle à manger en haut des marches.

BUENOS AIRES
OLIVOS, ARGENTINA

OWNERS Mercedes Hernáez & Alejandro Sticotti **OCCUPATION** Graphic designer &
Architect/designer **PROPERTY** House, 250 sqm/2,691 sq ft gross floor; 3 floors; 5 rooms;
5 bathrooms **YEAR** Building: 2007 **ARCHITECT** Alejandro Sticotti, www.sticotti.net
PHOTOGRAPHER Ricardo Labougle, www.ricardolabougle.com
PHOTO PRODUCER Ana Cardinale, www.anacardinale.com

This house has rigorous lines and was built with the utmost respect for nature. Its owner even recycled the wooden crates he used when moving back to Argentina from the States and incorporated them into its construction.
Das Haus besticht durch strenge Linien und wurde mit äußerstem Respekt vor der Natur gebaut. Sein Besitzer hat sogar die Holzkisten recycelt, die er für seinen Umzug aus den Vereinigten Staaten zurück nach Argentinien verwendete, und sie in den Bau integriert.
Cette maison aux lignes strictes et rigoureuses a été construite dans le plus grand respect de la nature. Le propriétaire a même recyclé les caisses en bois de son déménagement depuis les Etats-Unis et les a intégrées dans la structure.

P. 124 The owner and architect Alejandro Sticotti avoided felling a single tree to make way for the building. The structure on the upper levels is faced with lapacho wood. • Besitzer und Architekt Alejandro Sticotti hat für den Zugang zum Haus nicht einen einzigen Baum gefällt. Die Außenwände des oberen Stockwerks sind mit Lapachoholz verkleidet. • Le propriétaire, l'architecte Alejandro Sticotti, n'a pas abattu un seul arbre pour faire de la place au bâtiment. Les étages supérieurs sont tapissés de bardeaux en lapacho.

P. 125 Both the vintage metal chairs and standard lamp on the terrace date from the 1960s. • Sowohl die alten Metallsessel als auch die Lampe auf der Terrasse stammen aus den 1960ern. • Les sièges en métal et le lampadaire sur la terrasse datent des années 1960.

← Potted cacti add a sculptural element to the garden. • Eingetopfte Kakteen bilden ein skulpturales Element im Garten. • Des cactus en pot créent un élément sculptural dans le jardin.

"I built the house in a style that respected the trees and the immediate vicinity."

„Ich habe das Haus in einem Stil gebaut, der die Bäume und die unmittelbare Umgebung respektiert."
« J'ai construit la maison avec une esthétique respectant les arbres et l'environnement immédiat. »

P. 127 The "Cubo" sofa in the living room is sold at Sticotti's furniture gallery Net in the Palermo Viejo district of Buenos Aires. The wooden coffee table was made by antique dealer and designer Ricardo Paz and the "Butterfly" chair designed by Ferrari-Hardoy, Kurchan and Bonet in the 1930s. • Das „Cubo"-Sofa im Wohnzimmer wird in Sticottis Möbelgalerie Net im Bezirk Palermo Viejo in Buenos Aires verkauft. Der hölzerne Couchtisch wurde von dem Antiquitätenhändler und Designer Ricardo Paz designt; der „Butterfly"-Sessel ist ein Entwurf von Ferrari-

Hardoy, Kurchan und Bonet aus den 1930ern. • Dans le séjour, le canapé « Cubo » fait partie des meubles que Sticotti vend chez Net, sa boutique située dans le quartier de Palermo Viejo à Buenos Aires. La table basse en bois a été créée par le designer et antiquaire Ricardo Paz. Le fauteuil « Butterfly » a été dessiné par Ferrari-Hardoy, Kurchan et Bonet dans les années 1930.

← A stone fireplace takes centre stage in the double-height living room. • Ein Steinkamin bildet den Mittelpunkt des zweigeschossigen Wohnzimmers. •

Une cheminée en pierre occupe la place d'honneur dans le séjour qui possède une double hauteur sous plafond.

↑ On the ground floor, Sticotti created one large open space that flows out onto the surrounding terrace. • Im Erdgeschoss konzipierte Sticotti einen großen Raum, der sich zur Terrasse hin öffnet. • Au rez-de-chaussée, Sticotti a créé un grand espace ouvert qui fusionne avec la terrasse.

"Here, there is nothing predetermined and nothing pretentious."

„Hier gibt es nichts fest Vorgegebenes und nichts Prätentiöses."
« Ici, il n'y a rien de préétabli, rien de prétentieux. »

PP. 130–131 The lush vegetation around the house creates a wonderful sense of seclusion. • Die üppige Vegetation rund um das Haus schafft eine wunderbare Atmosphäre der Abgeschiedenheit. • La végétation dense autour de la maison crée une merveilleuse impression de solitude.

↑ Both the tables and storage units in the airy kitchen are topped with marble. • Sowohl die Tischplatten als auch die Schränke in der luftigen Küche sind aus Marmor. • Les tables et les placards de la cuisine lumineuse sont recouverts de plateaux de marbre.

→ The family labrador takes a nap at the bottom of the staircase, made from planks of wood and metallic tubes. The walls are concrete. • Der Labrador der Familie macht ein Nickerchen am Fuß der Treppe aus Holzbohlen und Metallrohren. Die Wände bestehen aus Beton. • Le labrador de la maison fait la sieste au pied de l'escalier réalisé avec des tubes métalliques et des planches en bois. Les murs sont en béton.

PP. 134–135 The deep sink is a custom design by Sticotti. The walls are clad with classic 10 x 10 cm white tiles. • Bei dem tiefen Spülbecken handelt es sich um eine Spezialanfertigung von Sticotti. Die Wände sind mit klassischen 10 x 10 cm großen Fliesen verkleidet. • L'évier profond a été dessiné par Sticotti. Les murs sont tapissés de carreaux blancs classiques de 10 x 10 cm.

↑ The dining table originally belonged to a school. The standard lamp is an industrial prototype from the 1960s. • Der Esstisch des Hauses stammt ursprünglich aus einer Schule. Die Steh-

lampe ist ein Prototyp aus den 1960ern. • La table provient à l'origine d'une école. Le lampadaire est un prototype industriel des années 1960.

→ The cooker is a rehabilitated industrial model from the 1960s. The vintage ceiling light was found at a Buenos Aires flea market. • Der Herd ist ein aufgearbeitetes Großküchenmodell aus den 1960ern. Die alte Deckenleuchte fand Sticotti auf dem Flohmarkt in Buenos Aires. • La cuisinière est un modèle industriel des années 1960 modernisé. Le plafonnier a été déniché sur le marché aux puces de Buenos Aires.

PP. 138–139 The furniture in the master bedroom was rescued from old warehouses. The cabinet on the right no doubt once belonged to a shop. • Die Möbel im Hauptschlafzimmer sind Fundstücke aus alten Lagerhäusern. Die Schubladenkommode rechts stand zweifellos einmal in einem Geschäft. • Les meubles de la chambre principale ont été récupérés dans de vieux entrepôts. Le présentoir sur la droite se trouvait sans doute dans une boutique.

PP. 140–141 Recycled pine wood was used on the wall behind the master bed. A vintage lamp bought in New York stands on a bedside table sold through Sticotti's gallery, Net. • Für die Wand hinter dem Bett wurde recyceltes Kiefernholz verwendet. Daneben steht eine alte Leselampe aus New York auf einem Nachttisch, der in Sticottis Galerie Net erhältlich ist. • Derrière le lit de la chambre principale, une cloison réalisée avec des planches de sapin recyclées. Une lampe vintage achetée à New York

est posée sur la table de chevet, un modèle vendu chez Net, la galerie de Sticotti.

↑ The woollen pouf is the "Sweet 40" model designed by Martin Churba for Gervasoni. • Bei dem Bodenkissen aus Wolle handelt es sich um das Modell „Sweet 40" von Martin Churba für Gervasoni. • Le pouf en laine « Sweet 40 » a été conçu par Martin Churba pour Gervasoni.

→ The purity of the structure's forms is offset by the profusion of vegetation surrounding it. • Die Klarheit der Formen des Gebäudes steht im Kontrast zu der üppigen Vegetation seiner Umgebung. • Les formes pures de la structure sont contrebalancées par la végétation luxuriante qui l'entoure.

CAPRI
CAMPANIA, ITALY

OWNERS Susanne & Matteo Thun **OCCUPATION** Architects
PROPERTY House, 250 sqm/2,700 sq ft gross floor; 2 floors; 6 rooms;
6 bathrooms **YEAR** Building: 1945, Remodelling: 2008
ARCHITECT Matteo Thun and Partners, www.matteothun.com
PHOTOGRAPHER Hiepler & Brunier, www.hiepler-brunier.de
PHOTO STYLIST Stephan Meyer

Good interior design reflects the soul of a place. Here, it is meant to evoke a mix between the rural neighbourhood and the Capri of the 1960s as epitomised by Brigitte Bardot in the film "Le Mépris."

Gutes Innendesign spiegelt die Seele eines Ortes. In diesem Fall entstand eine Mischung aus der ländlichen Umgebung des Anwesens und dem Capri der 1960er, wie es von Brigitte Bardot in dem Film „Die Verachtung" unsterblich gemacht wurde.

La décoration épouse l'âme du lieu. Ici, elle vise à conjuguer l'environnement champêtre et le Capri des années 1960 tel que l'incarne Brigitte Bardot dans « Le Mépris ».

"The view of the horizon hypnotises me."

„Der Blick auf den Horizont hypnotisiert mich."
« La vue de l'horizon m'hypnotise. »

PP. 144 The garden offers views over the bay of Marina Piccola. • Vom Garten aus überblickt man die Bucht von Marina Piccola. • Le jardin domine la baie de Marina Piccola.

P. 145 Perched above the pool is a shelter made from bamboo with a double bed for siestas. The ladders are used for drying swimsuits. • Oberhalb des Pools befindet sich eine kleine Hütte aus Bambus mit einem Doppelbett für Siestas. Die Leitern dienen zum Trocknen von Badesachen. • Perché au-dessus de la piscine, un abri en bambou avec un grand lit pour la sieste. Les échelles servent à faire sécher les maillots de bain.

P. 146–147 A view of the first-floor terrace with its banquette seating and vibrant bougainvillea. • Ansicht der Terrasse im ersten Stock mit ihrer steinernen Sitzbank und prachtvollen Bougainvilleen. • Une vue de la terrasse du premier étage, avec ses banquettes et ses bougainvillées éclatantes.

↑ The lemon grove with agapanthus and roses, where the Thuns play bowls. • Der Zitronenhain mit Agapanthus und Rosen, wo die Thuns Boule spielen. • La pergola, où les Thun jouent aux boules, est plantée de citronniers, d'agapanthes et de rosiers.

→ An outdoor table and bench are covered in tiles typical of the Amalfi Coast. This is where the couple entertain family and friends for lunch and dinner. • Der Tisch und die Bank im Freien sind mit den typischen Fliesen der Amalfiküste verkleidet. Mittags und abends bewirtet das Paar hier oft Familie und Freunde. • La table et le banc extérieurs sont recouverts de carreaux typiques de la côte amalfitaine. C'est ici que le couple déjeune et dîne avec la famille et les amis.

↑ The simple white furniture in the living room was made by local carpenters. • Die schlichten weißen Möbel im Wohnzimmer wurden von örtlichen Schreinern angefertigt. • Le mobilier blanc et sobre du séjour a été réalisé par des artisans locaux.

→ A window provides a glimpse of the swimming pool from the main living room. The glass vases on the ledge were created by Ettore Sottsass for Memphis. • Vom großen Wohnzimmer aus blickt man durch ein Fenster auf den Pool. Die Glasvasen auf der Fensterbank entwarf

Ettore Sottsass für Memphis. • Dans le grand séjour, une ouverture donne sur la piscine. Les vases en verre sur le rebord de la fenêtre ont été dessinés par Ettore Sottsass pour Memphis.

PP. 152–153 The walls of the main kitchen are covered with playful patchworks of tiles from L'Antica Ceramica. The vintage chandelier is Venetian. • Die Wände der Küche sind mit einem verspielten Patchwork aus Keramikfliesen von L'Antica Ceramica geschmückt. An der Decke hängt ein alter venezianischer Kronleuchter. • Les murs de la grande cuisine sont tapissés d'un joyeux patchwork de carreaux provenant de L'Antica Ceramica. Le lustre rétro est vénitien.

← The bedspread in Susanne Thun's room is made from Dedar fabrics.

The armchair is from an antique store in Milan called L'Oro dei Farlocchi. • Die Tagesdecke in Susanne Thuns Zimmer wurde aus Stoffen von Dedar angefertigt. Der Sessel stammt aus dem Mailänder Antiquitätengeschäft L'Oro dei Farlocchi. • Dans la chambre de Susanne Thun, le dessus-de-lit a été réalisé avec des tissus de Dedar. Le fauteuil a été acheté chez L'Oro dei Farlocchi, un antiquaire milanais.

↑ In son Constantin's room is a vintage travel bed covered with Rubelli textiles. • Im Zimmer von Sohn Constantin steht

ein altes Reisebett, bezogen mit Stoffen von Rubelli. • Dans la chambre du fils, Constantin, un ancien lit de voyage tapissé de tissus de Rubelli.

PP. 156–157 The all-white master bedroom offers a view of the famous Faraglioni rocks. • Vom ganz in Weiß gehaltenen Schlafzimmer aus hat man einen Blick auf die berühmten Felsformationen Faraglioni vor Capri. • Depuis la chambre principale, toute blanche, on aperçoit les célèbres rochers Faraglioni.

COHINIAC
BRITTANY, FRANCE

OWNERS Paola & Gianni Basso **OCCUPATION** Photographer
PROPERTY House, 250 sqm/2,700 sq ft gross floor; 3 floors; 6 rooms; 3 bathrooms
YEAR Building: 1840 **PHOTOGRAPHER** Gianni Basso/Vega MG, www.vegamg.it

An old presbytery turned into a very personal home with numerous flea market finds from Brittany. The rustic quality of the interiors was maintained and the colours inspired by those of the local boats.
Ein altes Pfarrhaus in der Bretagne wurde mithilfe vieler Flohmarktfunde in ein äußerst individuelles Heim verwandelt. Dabei bewahrten die Besitzer die rustikale Atmosphäre des Hauses und ließen sich bei der Farbgebung von den Farbtönen der lokalen Fischerboote inspirieren.
Un ancien presbytère converti en une maison très personnelle remplie de trouvailles chinées dans des marchés aux puces de Bretagne. Les intérieurs ont été conservés rustiques et les couleurs s'inspirent des bateaux locaux.

P. 158 The house is a former presbytery in a small village of just 400 inhabitants. Basso changed the colour of the shutters from brown to blue. • Das ehemalige Pfarrhaus liegt in einem Dorf mit nur 400 Einwohnern. Die Bassos ließen die vormals braunen Fensterläden blau streichen. • La maison est un ancien presbytère situé dans un petit village qui ne compte que 400 habitants. Basso a repeint en bleu les volets autrefois marron.

P. 159 In front of the house stands a steel sculpture by French artist Annick Argant, who lives on the Île de Bréhat. • Vor dem Haus steht eine Stahlskulptur von Annick Argant, einer Künstlerin von der

Île de Bréhat. • Devant la maison, une sculpture de l'artiste française Annick Argant, qui vit sur l'île de Bréhat.

← The wood and stone fireplace in the kitchen is original to the house. Basso made the mirror himself. The lamp to the right is a Joe Colombo design. • Der Kamin in der Küche befand sich bereits im Haus. Der Spiegel über dem Kamin wurde von Basso selbst angefertigt, und die Lampe rechts ist ein Design von Joe Colombo. • La cheminée en bois et pierre de la cuisine est d'origine. Basso a réalisé lui-même le miroir. Le luminaire sur la droite est de Joe Colombo.

↑ A juxtaposition of different hues in the entrance hall. Basso was inspired by the colours of local boats. • Ein Nebeneinander verschiedener Farbtöne im Eingangsbereich. Basso ließ sich von den Farben der lokalen Boote inspirieren. • Différentes couleurs ont été juxtaposées dans l'entrée. Basso s'est inspiré des bateaux locaux.

PP. 162–163 The 19th-century table came from a flea market. • Der Tisch aus dem 19. Jahrhundert ist ein Fundstück vom Flohmarkt. • La table du 19e siècle vient d'un marché aux puces.

"Everything in the house is simple and easy."

„Alles im Haus ist schlicht und einfach."
« Tout dans la maison est simple et facile. »

↑ In the master bedroom, Basso left the stonework of the wall visible above the fireplace. • Basso beließ das Mauerwerk über dem Kamin im Hauptschlafzimmer unangetastet. • Dans la chambre principale, Basso a laissé des pierres apparentes au-dessus de la cheminée.

→ Sofia at an early 20th-century desk. On the wall is a photo of the sea taken by Basso. • Sofia sitzt an einem Tisch aus dem frühen 20. Jahrhundert. An der Wand ein Foto von Basso. • Sofia derrière un pupitre d'école du début du 20ᵉ siècle. Au mur, une photo de Basso.

PP. 166–167 Basso's wife Paola sits in front of the fireplace in the living room. Vico Magistretti chairs flank a bistro table. • Bassos Frau Paola vor dem Kamin im Wohnzimmer. Davor Stühle von Vico Magistretti. • La femme de Basso, Paola, assise devant la cheminée du séjour. Les chaises pliantes sont de Vico Magistretti.

↑ The curtains in Sofia's room were made by stringing together pieces of seaweed. The bed dates from the late 19th century. • Für die Vorhänge in Sofias Zimmer wurde Seetang aufgefädelt. Das Bett stammt aus dem späten 19. Jahrhundert. • Les rideaux de la chambre de Sofia sont faits d'algues enfilées. Le lit date de la fin du 19ᵉ siècle.

→ A guest room in the attic with a rocking chair. Basso made the mirror on the easel himself. • Ein Gästezimmer im Dachgeschoss mit einem Schaukelstuhl. Der Spiegel auf der Staffelei ist eine Eigenanfertigung von Basso. • Dans une chambre d'amis, un rocking-chair. Le miroir sur le chevalet a été réalisé par Basso.

PP. 170–171 Above the fireplace in the "Blue Room" are four images Basso took at Lake Louise in Canada; view of a guest room. The "Roberta" chair is from IKEA. The wooden lamp was made by Basso. • Über dem Kamin im „Blauen Zimmer" vier Fotos von Basso. Blick in eines der Gästezimmer. Die Holzlampe wurde von Basso selbst angefertigt. • Dans la « chambre bleue », quatre photos du lac Louise prises par Basso au Canada. La chambre d'amis. Chaise « Roberta » d'Ikea et lampe de Basso.

EAST HAMPTON
LONG ISLAND, NEW YORK, USA

OWNERS A European family **PROPERTY** House, 650 sqm/7,000 sq ft gross floor;
2 floors; 6 rooms; 7 bathrooms **YEAR** Building: 1910, Remodelling: 2008
PHOTOGRAPHER Simon Watson, www.simonwatson.com
PHOTO STYLIST Michael Reynolds, www.themagnetagency.com
PHOTO PRODUCER Mayer Rus

The house acts as a showcase for a deliberately provocative collection of art. According to the owners, the furnishings "don't relate to each other in an obvious way."
Ein Haus als Ausstellungsraum für eine provokante Kunstsammlung. Die Eigentümer erzählen, dass sich die Einrichtungsgegenstände „nicht bewusst aufeinander beziehen".
Une maison qui sert de vitrine à une collection d'art délibérément provocante. Selon les propriétaires, le choix du mobilier « ne suit aucune logique particulière ».

P. 172 The classical façade of the 1910 house. • Die klassizistischen Fassade des 1910 erbauten Hauses. • La façade classique datant de 1910.

P. 173 An imposing sculpture by Jeff Koons stands guard by the pool. Entitled "Elephant," it is made from high-chromium stainless steel with a translucent pink finish. • Eine imposante Skulptur von Jeff Koons wacht über den Pool: Der „Elephant" ist aus Edelstahl mit hohem Chromhgehalt mit transparentem Finish in Pink gefertigt. • Une imposante sculpture de Jeff Koons monte la garde devant la piscine. Intitulée « Elephant », elle est en acier inoxydable à forte

teneur en chrome recouvert d'un vernis rose translucide.

PP. 174–175 The foyer features a console, armchairs and an opulent mirror; in the sunroom, Jorge Pardo pendants hang above a table and armchairs created by Franz West. • Das Foyer mit einer Konsole, Sesseln und einem opulenten Spiegel; im Wintergarten hängen Leuchten von Jorge Pardo über einem Tisch und Sesseln von Franz West. • L'entrée avec une console, des fauteuils et un miroir opulent ; dans le salon vitré, des plafonniers de Jorge Pardo sont suspendus audessus d'une table et de fauteuils créés par Franz West.

↑ A bench by Takashi Murakami and a custom coffee table and sofa in the living room. • Eine Sitzbank von Takashi Murakami sowie ein Couchtisch und ein Sofa im Wohnzimmer. • Dans le séjour, un banc de Takashi Murakami côtoie une table basse et un canapé réalisés sur mesure.

→ A Juergen Teller portrait of Barbara Cartland. • Ein Fotoporträt der Schriftstellerin Barbara Cartland von Juergen Teller. • Portrait de Barbara Cartland par Juergen Teller.

ESPOO
HELSINKI, FINLAND

OWNERS Olavi Koponen **OCCUPATION** Arts professor
PROPERTY House, 231 sqm/2,490 sq ft gross floor; 2 floors; 1–5 rooms; 2 bathrooms
YEAR Building: 2006 **ARCHITECT & INTERIOR DESIGNER** Olavi Koponen
PHOTOGRAPHER Toni Meneguzzo/GMAimages, www.tonimeneguzzo.com

Known as Kotilo "The Seashell House," this private residence is all about spatial experience. Its heart is a fireplace around which almost all the zones of the house twist. The result is quirky open volumes and a strong organic feel.
Kotilo oder das „Muschelhaus" ist ein Privathaus, bei dem es um Raumerfahrung geht. Den Mittelpunkt bildet eine Feuerstätte, um die sich fast alle Zonen des Hauses gruppieren. Das Ergebnis sind offene Räume und eine organische Atmosphäre.
Baptisée Kotilo, « la maison coquillage », cette résidence s'enroule autour d'une cheminée qui constitue son cœur. Elle offre une autre manière de vivre l'espace, toute en volumes ouverts et recoins excentriques, dégageant une forte impression organique.

P. 178 The idea for the shape of the house came to Olavi Koponen when he bent a polystyrene bar around a column. Its exterior is clad with larch shingles from Siberia. • Olavi Koponen hatte die Idee für die Form des Hauses, als er ein Stück Polystyrol um eine Säule bog. Die Außenverkleidung besteht aus sibirischen Lärchenschindeln. • Olavi Koponen a eu l'idée de donner cette forme à la maison en pliant une barre en polystyrène autour d'une colonne. L'extérieur est tapissé de bardeaux en mélèze de Sibérie.

P. 179 On the first-floor terrace, the owner has placed a series of Verner Panton's moulded plastic "Panto Pop" chairs. • Auf die Terrasse im ersten Stock hat der Eigentümer „Panto Pop"-Hocker aus Kunststoff von Verner Panton gestellt. • Sur le balcon, le propriétaire a placé des sièges en plastique moulé « Panto Pop » de Verner Panton.

↑ The kitchen is situated near the main entrance. • Der Küchenbereich liegt unmittelbar neben dem Haupteingang. • La cuisine est située près de l'entrée principale.

→ The internal spaces wrap around the central fireplace. A "Halo" ceiling light by Koizumi hangs above a concrete and recycled glass table. • Die Innenräume schlängeln sich um die zentrale Feuerstätte. Eine „Halo"-Leuchte von Koizumi hängt über einem Tisch aus Beton und recyceltem Glas. • Les espaces intérieurs s'enroulent autour de la cheminée centrale. Plafonnier « Halo » de Koizumi au-dessus d'une table en béton et en verre recyclé.

PP. 182–183 A "Rollo Chrom" sofa bed from Innovation on the upper floor. All the interior walls are covered with Finnish aspen. • Ein „Rollo Chrom"-Sofabett von Innovation im Obergeschoss. Alle Innenwände sind mit finnischem Espenholz verkleidet. • A l'étage, un canapé-lit « Rollo Chrom » de chez Innovation. Tous les murs intérieurs sont lambrissés en tremble finlandais.

← A view of the main entrance to the house with one of Arne Jacobsen's iconic "Egg" chairs in the background and a sculpture by Antero Koskinen. • Ansicht des Haupteingangs. Im Hintergrund Arne Jacobsens legendärer „Egg"-Sessel und eine Skulptur von Antero Koskinen. • Une vue de l'entrée principale avec une sculpture d'Antero Koskinen et, au fond, le célèbre fauteuil « Egg » d'Arne Jacobsen.

→ The free-standing shower unit was made with steel mesh and gypsum. The mosaic tiles are from Marazzi. • Die frei stehende Duschkabine wurde aus Baustahlmatten und Gips errichtet. Die Mosaikfliesen stammen von Marazzi. • La cabine de douche a été réalisée avec un treillis en acier et du plâtre. Le carrelage vient de chez Marazzi.

"The overall goal was simplicity and relaxed living."

„Das Hauptziel war Schlichtheit und Entspannung."
« L'idée était de créer une ambiance dépouillée dans laquelle il fait bon vivre. »

FRANKFURT

HESSEN, GERMANY

OWNER Bernd Hollin **OCCUPATION** Architect
PROPERTY Penthouse, 140 sqm/1,500 sq ft gross floor; 1 floor;
3 rooms; 2 bathrooms **YEAR** Building: 1958, Remodelling: 2004
INTERIOR DESIGNER Bernd Hollin, Hollin + Radoske, www.hollinradoske.de
PHOTOGRAPHER Ludger Paffrath, www.ludger-paffrath.de
PHOTO PRODUCER Andreas Tölke

A synthesis of a classic modern apartment of the late 1950s and the owner's contemporary, minimalistic design. The pure approach means no artwork, no handles on cupboards. The presence of two atriums and a loggia allow inside and outside spaces to merge.
Eine Synthese aus einem klassisch-modernen Apartment der späten 1950er und dem zeitgenössischen minimalistischen Design des Besitzers. Der puristische Ansatz bedeutet: keine Kunstwerke und keine Griffe an den Schränken.
Synthèse de l'appartement classique moderne de la fin des années 1950 et du design contemporain minimaliste du propriétaire. Son approche puriste se traduit par l'absence d'œuvres d'art et de poignées aux placards.

P. 186 A view towards the living room from the black slate jacuzzi in one of the two atriums. • Blick vom Jacuzzi aus schwarzem Schiefer in eines der beiden Atrien und ins Wohnzimmer. • Une vue du séjour depuis le jacuzzi en ardoise noire dans l'un des deux atriums.

P. 187 The Frankfurt cityscape can be admired from the front loggia. The outdoor wooden light fixtures were designed by Hollin + Radoske. • Von der vorderen Loggia aus kann man die Frankfurter Stadtlandschaft bewundern. Die Außenleuchten aus Holz wurden von Hollin + Radoske entworfen. • De la loggia, on peut admirer la vue sur Francfort. Les luminaires en bois ont été dessinés par Hollin + Radoske.

PP. 188–189 Leather cushions by Albrecht Ollendiek flank the low table in the living room. The red vases are from Zanotta. • Lederkissen von Albrecht Ollendiek flankieren den niedrigen Tisch im Wohnzimmer. Die roten Vasen stammen von Zanotta. • Dans le séjour, des coussins en cuir d'Albrecht Ollendiek entourent la table basse. Les vases rouges viennent de chez Zanotta.

← Eames chairs and a solid Portuguese slate table in the kitchen. • Eames-Stühle und ein Tisch mit massiver Schieferplatte in der Küche. • Dans la cuisine, des chaises Eames autour d'une robuste table portugaise en ardoise.

↑ Redaelli linen on the custom master bed. • Bettwäsche von Redaelli auf dem maßgefertigen Bett im Schlafzimmer. • Sur le lit réalisé sur mesure, du linge de chez Redaelli.

PP. 192–193 Beyond the koi pool, an armchair from Jeffrey Bernett's "Metropolitan" collection for B&B Italia stands on a "Fogg" rug from Kasthall. • Hinter dem Koi-Becken steht ein Sesselentwurf von Jeffrey Bernett für B&B Italia aus der „Metropolitan"-Kollektion auf einem „Fogg"-Teppich von Kasthall. • De l'autre côté du bassin koi, un fauteuil appartenant à la collection « Metropolitan » dessinée par Jeffrey Bernett pour B&B Italia sur un tapis « Fogg » de chez Kasthall.

GHENT
EAST FLANDERS, BELGIUM

OWNERS Bep De Reu & Dieter Van Everbroeck **OCCUPATION** Chemist & Architect
PROPERTY Pavilion house, 300 sqm/3,200 sq ft gross floor; 1 floor;
10 rooms; 1 bathroom **YEAR** Building: 1963, Remodelling: 2006
ARCHITECT & INTERIOR DESIGNER Dieter Van Everbroeck, B5architecten,
www.b5architecten.be **PHOTOGRAPHER** Frederik Vercruysse, www.frederikvercruysse.com
PHOTO PRODUCER Hilde Bouchez

A "banal 1960s bungalow" transformed into a sleek modernist house. Its focal point is a beech tree. In response to its verticality, architect Van Everbroeck stretched the structure horizontally.
Ein „banaler Bungalow aus den 1960ern" wurde in ein elegantes modernistisches Haus verwandelt. Den Blickfang des Geländes bildet eine Buche, deren Vertikalität im Kontrast zur horizontalen Ausdehnung des Baus steht.
Un « banal bungalow des années 1960 » transformé en maison moderniste. Son point de convergence, un hêtre tricentenaire. En réponse à sa verticalité, l'architecte Dieter Van Everbroeck a étiré la structure horizontalement.

P.194   The house is situated in the shade of a 300-year-old beech tree. Much is made of the interplay between the inside and outside. • Das Haus liegt im Schatten einer 300 Jahre alten Buche. Besonderes Augenmerk wurde auf das Wechselspiel zwischen innen und außen gelegt. • La maison est située sous un hêtre vieux de trois cents ans. L'interaction entre l'extérieur et l'intérieur a été exploitée au maximum.

P.195   According to the architect and owner Dieter Van Everbroeck, "walking along the glass wall makes you feel like a beachcomber strolling along the water line." • „Wenn man an der Glaswand entlanggeht, kommt man sich vor wie ein Strandgutsammler, der am Ufer herumstreift", so der Architekt und Be-

sitzer Dieter Van Everbroeck. • Selon l'architecte et propriétaire Dieter Van Everbroeck, « quand vous marchez le long du mur de verre, vous avez l'impression d'être à la plage, vous promenant au bord de l'eau ».

←   Polished concrete was used for the floors. The aluminium posts were painted black "to give a more graphic effect." • Für die Böden wurde polierter Beton verwendet. Die Aluminiumpfosten ließ Van Everbroeck schwarz streichen, „um eine stärkere plastische Wirkung zu erzielen". • Les sols sont en béton poli. Les poteaux en aluminium ont été peints en noir pour « un effet plus graphique ».

↑   Colour was used as a code throughout. Hues from Le Corbusier's 1931 colour collection were chosen for free-standing elements. • Im ganzen Haus ist Farbe wie ein Code eingesetzt: So wurden für die frei stehenden Elemente Töne aus Le Corbusiers Farbskala von 1931 verwendet. • La couleur a été utilisée comme un code dans toute la maison. Les éléments autonomes ont été peints dans des tons choisis dans le nuancier conçu par Le Corbusier en 1931.

PP.198–199   An orange dividing wall magnifies the effect of the setting sun. • Für eine Trennwand fiel die Wahl auf Orange, um den Effekt der untergehenden Sonne zu verstärken. • Le mur de séparation a été peint en orange pour magnifier l'effet du soleil couchant.

↑ Villeroy & Boch sinks and Grohe
taps in the bathroom. • Waschbecken
von Villeroy & Boch und Wasserhähne
von Grohe im Bad. • Les lavabos
viennent de chez Villeroy & Boch et
la robinetterie de chez Grohe.

→ Birch plywood units in the kitchen.
The blue is that used by Le Corbusier in
the corridor of the Villa Savoye. • Elemente aus Birkensperrholz in der Küche.
Das Blau entspricht dem Farbton, den Le
Corbusier im Korridor der Villa Savoye
verwendete. • Les placards de la cuisine
sont en bouleau. Le bleu est celui utilisé
par Le Corbusier dans le couloir de la
Villa Savoye.

↑ In the private office, an industrial light fixture is mounted on an aluminium post. • Im Arbeitszimmer ist eine Industrielampe an einen Aluminiumpfosten montiert. • Dans le bureau, une lampe industrielle a été montée sur un poteau en aluminium.

→ At one end of the living room is a desk created by placing a wooden door on trestles. • Der Schreibtisch an einem Ende des Wohnzimmers besteht aus einer umfunktionierten Holztür auf Böcken. • Dans un coin du séjour, un bureau a été créé en posant une vieille porte sur des tréteaux.

PP. 204–205 A tropical hardwood, louro gamela, was used to clad the façade. • Für die Verkleidung der Fassade wurde das Tropenholz Louro gamela verwendet. • La façade est tapissée de bardeaux de bois dur tropical appelé louro gamela.

GUARUJÁ
SÃO PAULO, BRAZIL

OWNERS Arthur Casas **OCCUPATION** Architect
PROPERTY Villa, 450 sqm/4,850 sq ft gross floor; 2 floors;
4 rooms; 4 bathrooms **YEAR** Building: 2005
ARCHITECT & INTERIOR DESIGNER Arthur Casas, www.arthurcasas.com
PHOTOGRAPHER Tuca Reinés, www.tucareines.com.br

In the middle of the Amazonian forest, Casas has built a symmetrical house consisting of an open living room flanked by cubes housing the private rooms. Particular emphasis was placed on the abolition of boundaries between the interior and exterior.

Mitten im Amazonas-Urwald hat Casas ein symmetrisches Haus gebaut, das aus einem offenen Wohnzimmer und zwei seitlichen Kuben besteht, in denen die Schlafzimmer untergebracht sind. Dem Besitzer ging es vor allem darum, Begrenzungen aufzuheben.

Au milieu de la forêt amazonienne, Casas a construit une maison symétrique composée d'un espace ouvert flanqué de cubes abritant les appartements privés. L'accent a été mis sur l'abolition des frontières entre l'intérieur et l'extérieur.

P. 206 Large windows make the living room completely transparent. The ceilings are 11 metres (36 feet) high. A suspended walkway connects the two wings on the upper floor. • Große Fenster machen das Wohnzimmer vollkommen transparent. Die Deckenhöhe beträgt elf Meter. Eine frei schwebende Brücke verbindet die beiden Flügel des Oberstocks. • Des baies vitrées rendent le séjour totalement transparent. La hauteur sous plafond est de 11 mètres. Une passerelle relie le premier étage avec les deux ailes.

P. 207 Cumaru wood was used to clad both the structure and the deck. The latter acts as a viewing platform to admire the surrounding Amazonian forest. • Für die Verkleidung des Hauses und der Terrasse wurde Cumaru-Holz verwendet. Die Terrasse dient als Aussichtsplattform, von der aus man den umliegenden Amazonas-Urwald bewundern kann. • Des lattes en cumaru tapissent les façades et la terrasse. Cette dernière sert de plateforme d'observation d'où on peut admirer la forêt environnante.

↖ The Casas-designed outdoor table has been paired with chairs from a store called Casual. • Der von Casas entworfene Tisch ist mit Stühlen von Casual, einem Händler von Outdoor-Möbeln, kombiniert. • Devant la table de jardin dessinée par Casas, deux chaises achetées dans une boutique baptisée Casual.

→ Two vintage 1960s chairs look out into the forest. • Zwei Stühle aus den 1960ern mit Blick auf den Urwald. • Deux fauteuils vintage des années 1960 orientés vers la forêt.

"For me, what counts most is the forest.
That's my passion."

„Mir geht es vor allem um den Wald. Das ist meine Leidenschaft."
« Pour moi, ce qui compte avant tout, c'est la forêt. C'est ma passion. »

← Casas designed the sofas and coffee table, the latter with 19th-century wood from farms. The steel chimney is from Fireorb. • Die Sofas und der Couchtisch sind Eigenkreationen von Casas, wobei das Holz für den Tisch von landwirtschaftlichen Anwesen des 19. Jahrhunderts stammt. Der hängende Kaminofen ist von Fireorb. • Casas a dessiné les canapés et la table basse. Cette dernière a été réalisée avec du bois récupéré dans des fermes du 19ᵉ siècle. La cheminée en acier vient de chez Fireorb.

↑ In the office, "Eames Aluminium Group" chairs stand at a lacquered MDF desk and drawing board. • „Eames Aluminium Group"-Stühle an einem lackierten MDF-Tisch und einem Zeichentisch im Arbeitszimmer. • Dans le bureau, des chaises « Aluminium Group » des Eames sont placées devant une table de travail et une planche à dessin en médium laqué.

↑ Among the objects on the shelves are a copy of a pre-Columbian sculpture and two Indonesian jars. • Im Büroregal stehen die Kopie einer präkolumbianischen Skulptur und zwei indonesische Gefäße. • Sur les étagères on voit une copie d'une sculpture précolombienne et deux flacons indonésiens.

→ The 1960s Martin Eisler armchair used to belong to Casas's grandmother. The cushions were made from fabrics found on travels to Peru, Morocco and Turkey. • Der Sessel von Martin Eisler aus den 1960ern gehörte Casas' Großmutter. Für die Kissen verwendete er Stoffe, die er auf Reisen entdeckte.

• Le fauteuil de Martin Eisler des années 1960 appartenait à la grand-mère de Casas. Les tissus des coussins ont été rapportés de ses voyages, notamment au Pérou, au Maroc et en Turquie.

IBIZA
BALEARIC ISLANDS, SPAIN

OWNER A publisher and organiser of art fairs
PROPERTY Villa, 440 sqm/4,740 sq ft gross floor; 2 floors; 5 rooms; 6 bathrooms
YEAR Building: 2009 **ARCHITECT** Andrés Jaque Arquitectos, www.andresjaque.net
INTERIOR DESIGNER Luis García Fraile **PHOTOGRAPHER** Belén Imaz/AD Spain
© Condé Nast España, S.A. **PHOTO PRODUCER** Isabel Margalejo

The "Never Never Land" house was built on a steep slope around the existing bushes and trees, many of which were integrated inside the house. The aim was to make the interiors warm and cosy, with rustic accents and wood.
Das „Never Never Land"-Haus entstand an einem Steilhang, wobei der vorhandene Baumbestand teilweise in das Innere integriert wurde. Das Interieur sollte warm und gemütlich ausfallen, mit rustikalen Akzenten und Holz.
Construite sur une pente escarpée, la maison « Never Never Land » a été conçue autour des buissons et des arbres dont beaucoup ont été intégrés dans la structure. L'intérieur devait être chaleureux et douillet, avec des accents rustiques et du bois.

P. 214 The house is deliberately open to the exterior. The inside was initially painted sky blue, but that proved too cold. A sea-like turquoise was chosen instead. • Das Haus war innen ursprünglich himmelblau gestrichen, was sich jedoch als zu kalt erwies. Stattdessen fiel die Wahl auf einen Türkiston, der der Farbe des Meeres gleicht. • La maison est délibérément ouverte sur l'extérieur. A l'origine, l'intérieur était peint d'un bleu ciel. Les propriétaires lui ont préféré un turquoise plus proche de la couleur de la mer.

P. 215 Several parts of the house are built on stilts. The two lower units are independent guest quarters, each with their own terrace. • Einige Teile des Hauses wurden auf Pfählen errichtet. Die beiden unteren Einheiten beherbergen voneinander unabhängige Gästebereiche, jeweils mit eigener Terrasse. • Certaines parties de la maison sont bâties sur pilotis. Les deux unités inférieures abritent des appartements indépendants pour les invités. Chacune possède sa propre terrasse.

← Wooden stools from the flea market and a set of "Lizz" chairs designed by Piero Lissoni for Kartell stand around an iron dining table by Nick Projects. The kitchen is from Zelari de Nuzzi. • Um einen Esstisch aus Eisen von Nick Projects sind Holzhocker vom Flohmarkt und vier „Lizz"-Stühle gruppiert, die Piero Lissoni für Kartell entwarf. Die Küche stammt von Zelari de Nuzzi. • Autour de la table en fer du coin repas de Nick Projects, des tabourets en bois chinés dans un marché aux puces et des

chaises « Lizz » dessinées par Piero Lissoni pour Kartell. La cuisine vient de chez Zelari de Nuzzi.

↑ A number of existing trees have been integrated into the interior of the house. A palm tree cuts through the living room. The wooden bench is from the Paris flea market and the pen drawing above the fireplace is by Miguel Ángel Rebollo (José Robles Art Gallery Madrid). • Teile des vorhandenen Baumbestands wurden in das Innere des Hauses inte-

griert – so durchschneidet eine Palme das Wohnzimmer. Die Holzbank stammt von einem Flohmarkt in Paris; über dem Kamin hängt eine Tuschzeichnung von Miguel Ángel Rebollo (José Robles Art Gallery Madrid). • Plusieurs arbres ont été intégrés dans la maison, dont ce palmier qui traverse le séjour. Le banc en bois vient d'un marché aux puces parisien et le dessin au crayon au-dessus de la cheminée est de Miguel Ángel Rebollo (José Robles Art Gallery Madrid).

PP. 218-219 A pair of iconic "Acapulco" chairs, originally designed in the 1950s, stand in the living room. The loungers by the pool were designed by Luis García Fraile. • Im Wohnzimmer stehen zwei „Acapulco"-Stühle, Neuauflagen der Originale aus den 1950ern. Die Liegen am Pool stammen vom spanischen Innendesigner Luis García Fraile. • Une paire de sièges « Acapulco », rééditions de l'original dessiné dans les années 1950. Les lits au bord de la piscine ont été conçus par Luis García Fraile.

↑ → In the bathroom, a pair of "Tolomeo" lights hang above an IKEA mirror; the ceramic stool is from Asiatides. A cheeky photo of a swimmer has been applied to one of the glass walls of the shower. • Über einem IKEA-Spiegel im Bad hängen „Tolomeo"-Leuchten; der Keramikhocker ist von Asiatides. Auf eine der Glaswände der Dusche wurde augenzwinkernd das Foto einer Schwimmerin aufgebracht. • Dans la salle de bain, deux lampes « Tolomeo » sont accrochées au-dessus d'un miroir Ikea ; le tabouret en céramique vient de chez Asiatides. Une photo coquine de nageuse a été appliquée sur une des parois en verre de la douche.

IBIZA
BALEARIC ISLANDS, SPAIN

OWNER Victor Esposito **OCCUPATION** Interior designer
PROPERTY Villa 355 sqm/3,820 sq ft gross floor; 1 floor; 9 rooms; 3 bathrooms
YEAR Building: 17th century, Remodelling: 2005 **ARCHITECT** Pascal Cheikh Djavadi
Atelier Arcos Architecture, www.arcosarchitecture.fr **INTERIOR DESIGNER** Victor Esposito
PHOTOGRAPHER Matthieu Salvaing, www.matthieusalvaing.com
PHOTO PRODUCER Jérôme Dion

A 17th-century finca was extended in order to create a striking, Modernist villa. Inside, the keywords are simplicity and minimalism. The neutral framework allows the owner to change the decoration often.
Eine Finca aus dem 17. Jahrhundert wurde erweitert und zu einer beeindruckenden modernistischen Villa umgebaut. Im Inneren dominieren Schlichtheit und Minimalismus. Der neutrale Rahmen ermöglicht es dem Besitzer, die Dekoration regelmäßig zu verändern.
Une finca du 17e siècle agrandie pour créer une saisissante villa moderniste. A l'intérieur, les mots d'ordre sont simplicité et minimalisme. Le cadre neutre permet au propriétaire de changer souvent de décor.

"My goal is always to preserve traditional elements of architecture and combine them with modern influences."

„Mir geht es immer darum, traditionelle architektonische Elemente zu bewahren und sie mit modernen Einflüssen zu kombinieren."
« Mon objectif est de toujours préserver les éléments traditionnels de l'architecture et de les associer à des influences modernes. »

P. 222 A centuries-old olive tree presides in front of the sitting room. • Ein jahrhundertealter Olivenbaum ragt vor dem Wohnzimmer auf. • Un olivier plusieurs fois centenaire se dresse devant le salon.

P. 223 A 20-metre (66-foot) lap pool was built, although the house has no running water. Instead, it has a cistern, which is filled by lorry. • Auch wenn es kein fließendes Wasser im Haus gibt, ließ Esposito einen 20 Meter langen Pool

bauen. Die Wasserversorgung erfolgt über eine Zisterne, die von einem Tankwagen gefüllt wird. • Un couloir de nage de 20 mètres de long a été construit bien que la maison n'ait pas l'eau courante. Elle possède néanmoins une citerne remplie par camion.

→ A DS-600 leather sofa, manufactured by de Sede in the 1970s, snakes its way across the living room. The words on the wall are the cryptic title of an exhibition at the Irish Museum of Modern Art

in Dublin. • Ein DS-600-Ledersofa von de Sede aus den 1970ern schlängelt sich durch das Wohnzimmer. Die Inschrift an der Wand ist der rätselhafte Titel einer Ausstellung im Irish Museum of Modern Art in Dublin. • Un canapé en cuir DS-600, édité par de Sede dans les années 1970, serpente dans le séjour. Les mots sur le mur reprennent l'intitulé énigmatique d'une exposition de l'Irish Museum of Modern Art de Dublin.

← ↑ The kitchen stands back-to-back
with a lacquered bookcase. • Die Kü-
chenzeile steht Rücken an Rücken mit
einem lackierten Bücherregal. • La
cuisine se trouve dos à dos avec la bibliothèque en bois laqué.

227

PP. 228-229 The dining table and chairs are Eero Saarinen prototypes. The artwork is by Michael Craig-Martin. • Der Esstisch und die Stühle sind Prototypen von Eero Saarinen. Das Kunstwerk stammt von Michael Craig-Martin. • Les chaises et la table de salle à manger sont des prototypes d'Eero Saarinen. Le tableau est de Michael Craig-Martin.

↑ → Galician stone covers the shower floor. The sheepskin throw was made by Mapuche Indians. • Der Boden im Bad ist mit Steinen aus Galicien gefliest. Die Schaffelldecke haben Mapuche-Indianer gefertigt. • Les dalles de la douche sont taillées dans une pierre de Galice. Le dessus-de-lit en peau de mouton a été réalisé par des Mapuches.

ISTANBUL
TURKEY

OWNER Serdar Gülgün **OCCUPATION** Art historian, designer & decorator
PROPERTY Apartment, 360 sqm/3,875 sq ft gross floor; 1 floor;
4 rooms; 3 bathrooms **YEAR** Building: late 19th century, Remodeling: 1995
INTERIOR DESIGNER Serdar Gülgün
PHOTOGRAPHER Reto Guntli/Zapaimages, www.retoguntli.com

In transforming a 19th-century stone palazzo apartment, Serdar Gülgün created an interior based on his vast collection of 18th- and 19th-century Ottoman art and furniture. The result is grand, unpretentious and timeless.
Serdar Gülgün baute eine Etage in einem osmanischen Palast aus dem 19. Jahrhundert um und schuf ein Interieur für seine umfangreiche Sammlung osmanischer Kunstwerke und Möbel aus dem 18. und 19. Jahrhundert. Das Ergebnis ist beeindruckend und unprätentiös.
Réaménageant un appartement situé dans un palais du 19ᵉ siècle, Serdar Gülgün a créé un décor centré autour de sa vaste collection d'œuvres d'art et de mobilier ottomans des 18ᵉ et 19ᵉ siècles. Le résultat est grandiose et sans prétention.

P. 232 A rare portrait of Sultan Abdülmecid dating from the 1850s has been mounted on a piece of 19th-century Ottoman embroidery. • Ein seltenes Porträt von Sultan Abdülmecid aus den 1850ern vor einer osmanischen Sticke-rei aus dem 19. Jahrhundert. • Un por-trait rare du sultan Abdülmecid datant des années 1850, monté sur une étoffe ottomane brodée du 19ᵉ siècle.

P. 233 The balcony overlooks the Italian embassy and a garden with magnolia trees. The turtle-shaped candle holders were designed by Gülgün. • Der Balkon geht auf einen Garten mit Magnolien-bäumen. Die Schildkröten-Kerzenhalter sind Eigenentwürfe von Gülgün. • Le balcon domine un jardin planté de mag-

nolias et un palais construit pour accueil-lir l'ambassade d'Italie. Les bougeoirs en forme de tortues sur la table ont été conçus par Gülgün.

↑ The two armchairs to the left are in the Napoleon III style. • Auf der linken Seite: zwei Sessel im Stil Napoléons III. • Sur la gauche, deux fauteuils Napoléon III.

→ A 18th-century throne is set in a wooden arch from an old Ottoman palace. The portrait represents the 15th-century Prince Cem. • Ein Thron aus dem 18. Jahrhundert vor einem Holzbogen aus einem osmanischen Palast. Das Porträt zeigt Prinz Cem, der im 15. Jahrhundert lebte. • Un

trône du 18ᵉ siècle placé sous une arche en bois provenant d'un vieux palais otto-man. Au centre, un portrait du prince Cem qui a vécu au 15ᵉ siècle.

PP. 236–237 In front of the window in the main sitting room is an important 18th-century Ottoman throne. On the coffee table is a collection of antique turbans. • Vor dem Fenster des Haupt-wohnzimmers steht ein eindrucksvoller osmanischer Thron aus dem 18. Jahr-hundert. Auf dem Couchtisch liegt eine Sammlung antiker Turbane. • Devant la fenêtre du grand salon, un imposant trône ottoman du 18ᵉ siècle. Sur la table basse, une collection de turbans anciens.

PP. 238–241 Stripes are a recurrent motif, whether on the "lit bateau" sofa in the guestroom or the walls of the corridor. • Das verbindende dekorative Motiv in der Wohnung sind Streifen – sei es auf dem „Lit bateau" im Gästezimmer oder an den Wänden der Diele. • Les rayures sont un thème récurrent, que ce soit sur le lit bateau converti en canapé dans la chambre d'amis ou les murs du couloir.

PP. 242–243 Antique helmet-shaped copper dishes and a Baccarat jardinière are used to decorate the dining table. • Antike, wie Helme geformte Speiseglocken aus Kupfer und eine Jardiniere aus Baccarat-Kristall zieren den Esstisch. • La table de la salle à manger est décorée de couvre-plats en cuivre en forme de casque et d'une jardinière en cristal de Baccarat.

PP. 244–245 The clock above the master bed is in the shape of the Ottoman imperial coat of arms. • Die Uhr über dem großen Bett hat die Form eines osmanischen Herrscherwappens. • L'horloge au-dessus du grand lit a la forme du blason impérial ottoman.

JOSHUA TREE
MOJAVE DESERT, CALIFORNIA, USA

OWNER Andrea Zittel **OCCUPATION** Artist **PROPERTY** House
80 sqm/860 sq ft gross floor; 1 floor; 4 rooms; 1 bathroom
YEAR Building: 1946, Remodelling: 2000-02 **INTERIOR DESIGNER** Andrea Zittel,
www.zittel.org **PHOTOGRAPHER** Bärbel Miebach, www.barbelmiebach.com

Andrea Zittel specialises in creating experimental living situations. Her 1940s homesteader's cabin on the outskirts of Joshua Tree provides a testing ground for her work. As she says, "Each piece inside was a project."
Die Künstlerin Andrea Zittel hat sich auf die Kreation experimenteller Wohnsituationen spezialisiert. Ihr zweites Zuhause – eine Siedlerhütte aus den 1940ern – dient ihr als Testgelände für ihre Arbeit. „Jedes Stück im Inneren war ein Projekt", so Zittel.
Andrea Zittel est spécialisée dans la création d'espaces de vie expérimentaux. Sa résidence secondaire, une maison de colons des années 1940 près de Joshua Tree, lui sert de terrain d'expérimentation. Comme elle le dit elle-même « chaque élément à l'intérieur a d'abord été un projet ».

P. 246 Objects assembled by one wall of the house. Among them, an animal skull, a geode and a small yellow stone painted by Zittel's grandmother. • Entlang der Hauswand ausgelegte Objekte – ein Tierschädel, eine Geode und ein kleiner gelber Stein, der von Zittels Großmutter bemalt wurde. • Des objets assemblés au pied d'un mur de la maison. Parmi eux, un crâne de cerf, une géode et un caillou jaune peint par la grand-mère de Zittel.

P. 247 The 1940s homesteader's cabin stands on 25 acres and has been extended over the years. Zittel refers to it as "a weird modernist shack." • Die Siedlerhütte steht auf einem 10 Hektar großen Grundstück und wurde im Laufe der Jahre erweitert. Zittel bezeichnet sie als „eine eigentümlich modernistische Baracke". • Se dressant sur un terrain de 10 hectares, la maison de colons des années 1940 a été agrandie au fil des ans. Zittel la qualifie « d'étrange cabane moderniste ».

P. 248–249 Zittel is sitting on a multi-purpose piece of furniture made from charcoal foam entitled "Raugh." The front part acts as a bench and the back as a desk. • Zittel sitzt auf einem Multifunktionsmöbel aus anthrazitfarbenem Schaumstoff, das sie „Raugh" nennt. Der vordere Teil dient als Bank, der hintere als Schreibtisch. • Zittel est assise sur un meuble polyvalent en mousse de charbon baptisé « Raugh ». La partie avant sert de banc et l'arrière de bureau.

↖ Zittel's son Emmett in the kitchen, which was originally commissioned by a museum in Napa. • Zittels Sohn Emmett in der Küche, die ursprünglich von einem Museum in Napa in Auftrag gegeben wurde. • Emmett, le fils de Zittel, dans la cuisine, à l'origine une commande d'un musée de Napa.

↑ The kitchen table incorporates a grill and built-in plates. • Der Küchentisch ist mit einem Grill versehen. Mulden dienen als eingebaute Teller. • La table de la cuisine possède un gril et des dépressions servant d'assiettes.

P. 252-253 A felt bowl stands on a laminated birch and foam coffee table. • Eine Filzschale auf einem Couchtisch aus laminierter Birke und Schaumstoff. • Une coupe en feutre sur une table basse en mousse et en contreplaqué de bouleau.

↑ A group of experimentations with paper pulp. • Einige Experimente mit Papiermasse. • Une série d'expériences avec de la pâte à papier.

↗ The office in the studio building. • Das Büro im Ateliertrakt. • Le bureau de Zittel dans son atelier.

→ Zittel created the crocheted bed cover and felt wall hanging. • Die ge-häkelte Tagesdecke und der Wand-behang aus Filz wurden von Zittel ent-worfen. • Le dessus-de-lit au crochet et le ta-bleau en feutre sont de Zittel.

PP. 256–257 Made from shipping containers, Zittel's studio wraps its way around a group of mesquite trees. • Das aus Schiffscontainern gebaute Atelier von Zittel umschließt eine Gruppe von Mesquite-Bäumen. • Construit avec des conteneurs, l'atelier de Zittel forme un U autour d'un groupe de prosopis.

← This trailer is part of an art project, "The A–Z Work Station." • Dieser Container ist Teil des Kunstprojekts „The A–Z Work Station". • Cette caravane fait partie d'un projet artistique intitulé « The A–Z Work Station ».

→ These small capsules are shelters for people to stay in. • Diese Kapseln sollen als Zufluchts- und Aufenthaltsorte dienen. • Ces petits modules servent d'abris habitables.

PP. 260–263 One of three trailers commissioned by the SFMoMA. This one was customised by Zittel's parents; the other images show shelters from "The A–Z Wagon Stations" series. • Einer der drei Container, die vom SFMoMA in Auftrag gegeben wurden. Die Ausgestaltung stammt von Zittels Eltern. Die anderen Bilder zeigen Container aus der Serie „The A–Z Wagon Stations". • L'une des trois caravanes commandées par le musée d'art moderne de San Francisco ; celle-ci a été customisée par les parents de Zittel. Les autres photos montrent des abris de la série « The A–Z Wagon Stations ».

"An ongoing endeavour to better understand human nature and the social construction of needs."

„Ein dauerhaftes Streben nach einem besseren Verständnis der menschlichen Natur und der sozialen Konstruktion von Bedürfnissen."
« Un projet en évolution constante pour mieux comprendre la nature humaine et la construction sociale des besoins. »

JOUARS-PONTCHARTRAIN
ÎLE-DE-FRANCE, FRANCE

OWNER Olivier Auclert **OCCUPATION** Stomatologist
PROPERTY House, 326 sqm/3,500 sq ft gross floor; 1 floor; 8 rooms; 4 bathrooms
YEAR Building: 1972–75, Remodelling: 2006 **ARCHITECT** Etienne Fromanger
PHOTOGRAPHER Xavier Béjot/Tripod Agency, www.xavierbejot.com
PHOTO PRODUCER Ian Phillips/Tripod Agency, www.tripodagency.com

This house is hidden underground in the middle of a forest. The current owner kept original fixtures and fittings from the 1970s, such as the cork and carpet on the walls, and added design classics by the likes of Charles and Ray Eames and Eero Saarinen.

Das weitgehend unterirdische Haus liegt mitten im Wald. Der heutige Besitzer beließ die Originalausstattung aus den 1970ern unverändert und ergänzte sie um Designklassiker von Charles und Ray Eames oder Eero Saarinen.

Une maison à demi enfouie sous terre au milieu d'une forêt. Le propriétaire a conservé l'aménagement intérieur des années 1970, y compris le liège et la moquette aux murs, et y a ajouté des classiques du design signés Charles et Ray Eames ou Eero Saarinen.

"I don't think it's nice to see houses in the middle of a forest. They ruin the landscape."

„Ich möchte mitten in einem Wald keine Häuser
sehen – sie ruinieren die Landschaft."

« Je n'aime pas voir des maisons au milieu d'une forêt.
Cela gâche le paysage. »

P. 264 Several rooms are illuminated by domed skylights, which appear above ground like glazed space pods. The grass roof has great insulating qualities. • Einige Räume werden durch gewölbte Oberlichter beleuchtet, die über der Erde wie verglaste Raumkapseln wirken. Das Grasdach sorgt für eine hervorragende Isolierung. • Plusieurs pièces sont éclairées par des tabatières arrondies qui, vues de l'extérieur, évoquent des nacelles spatiales. Le toit tapissé de gazon isole la maison.

P. 265 Covered with ivy, the house is situated on a 11-acre plot in the middle of a forest. Roe deer often come right up to the terrace. • Das von Efeu überwucherte Haus liegt auf einem 4,5 Hektar großen Grundstück mitten im Wald. Gelegentlich kommen Rehe bis auf die Terrasse. • Couverte de lierre, la maison se trouve sur un terrain de 4,5 hectares au milieu d'une forêt. Les chevreuils viennent souvent jusque sur la terrasse.

↖ View of one of the children's rooms. • Blick in eines der Kinderzimmer. • Une vue de la chambre des enfants.

→ The staircase of the entrance hall is clad in wenge. The corridor runs downhill to the living room to create a dramatic perspective. • Die Treppe zur Eingangshalle ist mit Wenge verkleidet. Der Korridor führt zum Wohnzimmer hinab und sorgt so für eine spektakuläre Perspektive. • L'escalier de l'entrée est tapissé de palissandre d'Afrique. Le couloir s'enfonce jusqu'au séjour, créant une perspective théâtrale.

↑ An IKEA shelving unit in the colourfully decorated master bedroom. • Ein IKEA-Regal im farbenfroh dekorierten Hauptschlafzimmer. • Une bibliothèque de chez Ikea dans la chambre principale décorée de couleurs vives.

→ One wall in the living room has been decorated with strips of coloured paper. The sofa is the "Tufty-Time" model, designed by Patricia Urquiola for B&B Italia. The coffee table is from Artelano. • Eine der Wände des Wohnzimmers ist mit bunten Papierstreifen dekoriert.

Beim Sofa handelt es sich um das Modell „Tufty-Time", das Patricia Urquiola für B&B Italia entwarf. Der Couchtisch stammt von Artelano. • Un mur du séjour est décoré de bandes de papier coloré. Le canapé « Tufty-Time » a été dessiné par Patricia Urquiola pour B&B Italia. La table basse vient de chez Artelano.

PP. 270-271 A set of "Panton" chairs designed by Verner Panton stand around the equally iconic "Tulip" dining table by Eero Saarinen. • „Panton"-Stühle von

Verner Panton stehen um den ebenso legendären „Tulip"- Esstisch von Eero Saarinen. • Un ensemble de chaises « Panton » dessinées par Verner Panton entoure la tout aussi célèbre table « Tulip » d'Eero Saarinen.

PP. 272-273 The house is constructed from a series of concrete vaults. • Das Haus besteht aus aneinandergereihten Betongewölben. • La maison est composée d'une enfilade de voûtes en béton.

← The original orange tiles of the kitchen were retained. The table is actually the "Ad Hoc" desk designed by Antonio Citterio for Vitra. The chairs were designed by Charles and Ray Eames and the bar stools are the "Hi-Pad" model by Jasper Morrison. • Die orangefarbenen Kacheln in der Küche gehörten zur Originalausstattung des Hauses. Der Schreibtisch „Ad Hoc" ist ein Entwurf von Antonio Citterio für Vitra. Die Stühle sind von Charles und Ray Eames, und die „Hi-Pad"-Barhocker gestaltete Jasper Morrison. • Dans la cuisine, le carrelage

orange d'origine a été conservé. Le bureau « Ad Hoc » dessiné par Antonio Citterio pour Vitra fait office de table. Les chaises sont de Charles et Ray Eames et les tabourets de bar « Hi-Pad » de Jasper Morrison.

↑ One wall of the dining room is decorated with a series of screen prints by Gérard Fromanger. • An einer Wand des Esszimmers hängen Siebdrucke von Gérard Fromanger. • Un mur de la salle à manger est tapissé de sérigraphies de Gérard Fromanger.

PP. 276–277 In the master suite, the bed and side tables are from Patricia Urquiola's "Fat-Fat" range. The duvet cover and pillow cases are from Sonia Rykiel. • Das Bett und die Nachttische im Schlafzimmer sind Möbel aus der Reihe „Fat-Fat" von Patricia Urquiola, die Decken- und Kissenbezüge von Sonia Rykiel. • Le lit et les tables de nuit de la chambre principale appartiennent à la ligne « Fat-Fat » de Patricia Urquiola. La housse de couette et les taies d'oreiller viennent de chez Sonia Rykiel.

LONDON
KNIGHTSBRIDGE, UK

OWNER Roland Emmerich **OCCUPATION** Film director **PROPERTY** House
390 sqm/4,200 sq ft gross floor; 6 floors; 15 rooms; 7 bathrooms
YEAR Building: c. 1820, Remodelling: 2008 **INTERIOR DESIGNER** John Teall,
Fluxinteriors, www.johnteall.com **PHOTOGRAPHER** Gavin Jackson/Arcaid Images,
www.arcaidimages.com **PHOTO PRODUCER & STYLIST** John Teall, Fluxinteriors

The house is subversive, eclectic and full of humour. "The idea," explains designer Teall, "was to provoke thought, amuse and maybe shock a little." Political art includes a mural of Mao and a model of Abu Ghraib prison.
Ein Haus voller Humor. „Es sollte zum Nachdenken anregen, erheitern und vielleicht auch ein wenig schockieren", so John Teall. Zu der politisch motivierten Kunst im Haus gehört auch ein Modell des Gefängnisses von Abu Ghraib.
Une maison éclectique et pleine d'humour. Le décorateur John Teall explique : « L'idée était de donner à réfléchir, d'amuser et, peut-être, de choquer un peu. » La collection d'art politiquement engagé inclut une maquette de la prison d'Abu Ghraib.

P. 278 At the entrance to the open living area, a bust of Stalin found on eBay looks over a Louis XVI chair cheekily painted with the monarch's image. • Am Eingang zum großen, offenen Wohnbereich blickt eine Stalin-Büste auf einen Louis-XVI-Stuhl, der mit dem Bild des französischen Herrschers bemalt ist. • A l'entrée du grand séjour ouvert, un buste de Staline acheté sur eBay surplombe un fauteuil Louis XVI sur lequel a été peint non sans insolence une effigie du monarque.

P. 279 Stuffed birds stand guard in the black lacquer kitchen from Tsunami. The painting, bought at auction in Russia, is one of several references to Communism. • Ausgestopfte Vögel stehen Wache in der schwarzen Lack-Küche von Tsunami. Das Gemälde ersteigerte

Emmerich bei einer Auktion in Russland. • Des oiseaux empaillés montent la garde dans la cuisine de chez Tsunami. Le tableau, acheté aux enchères en Russie, est l'une des nombreuses références au communisme dans la maison.

← A zebra from Deyrolle in Paris presides over the living room. The rug was commissioned from Deirdre Dyson. • Ein Zebra von Deyrolle in Paris dominiert das Wohnzimmer. Der Teppich wurde von Deirdre Dyson gefertigt. • Un zèbre provenant du taxidermiste parisien Deyrolle domine le séjour. Le tapis a été commandé à Deirdre Dyson.

↑ Glass coffee tables enclose models of politically significant places. Here, the Dallas street where JFK was shot. • In den vitrinenartigen Couchtischen sind

bedeutende politische Orte zu sehen. Hier die Straße in Dallas, in der JFK erschossen wurde. • Plusieurs tables basses en verre renferment des maquettes de lieux ayant une importance politique. Ici, l'avenue de Dallas où John F. Kennedy a été assassiné.

PP. 282–284 Political imagery abounds in the living room, from the mural of Mao to armchairs upholstered with Russian propaganda banners. • Im Wohnzimmer ist die politische Bildsprache überall präsent, von dem Mao-Wandbild bis zu den Sesseln mit russischen Propagandabannern. • L'iconographie politique abonde dans le séjour, de la fresque de Mao aux fauteuils tapissés de propagande russe.

"Nothing is spared, from government and gender
to race and religion – but there's no manifesto."

„Nichts wird verschont, von Regierungen und Geschlecht
bis zu Rasse und Religion. Aber es gibt kein Manifest."
« Rien n'a été épargné, de la politique à la sexualité,
de la race à la religion, mais il n'y a pas de manifeste. »

→ Under the stairs, a wax effigy of John
Paul II reads media coverage of his death.
• Unter der Treppe eine Wachsfigur von
Johannes Paul II., der Artikel über seinen
Tod liest. • Sous l'escalier, une statue en
cire de Jean-Paul II lisant sa nécrologie
dans la presse.

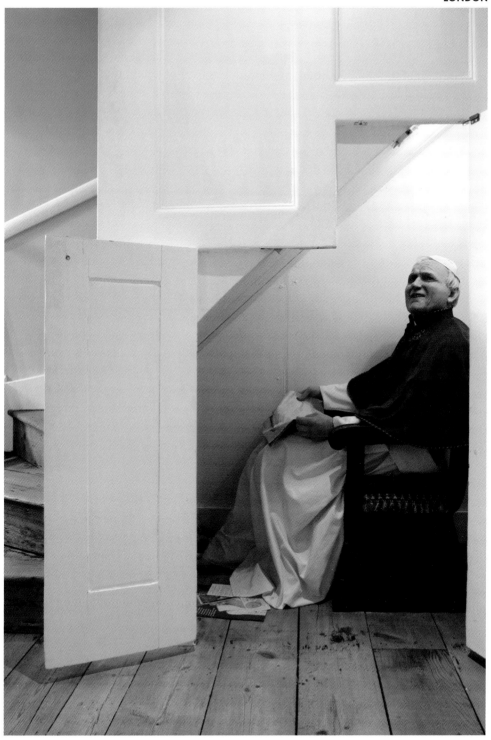

↑ The attic honours Francis Bacon with paintings of his studio. • Das Dachgeschoss ist eine Hommage an Francis Bacon. • Le grenier est un hommage à Francis Bacon.

PP. 287–291 A "God Bless America" shower curtain; an erect penis motif on the wall; a bird cage in the shape of the White House; antique flags from Lassco. • Ein Duschvorhang mit der Aufschrift „God Bless America", das Motiv eines erigierten Penis an der Wand, ein Käfig in Form des Weißen Hauses, antike Flaggen von Lassco. • Un rideau de douche : « Que Dieu bénisse l'Amérique » ; un papier peint avec des pénis en érection ; une cage à oiseaux reprenant la forme de la Maison Blanche ; des drapeaux anciens achetés chez Lassco.

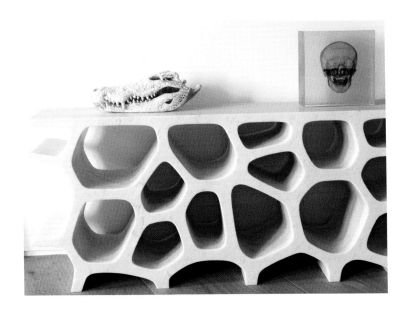

LONDON

ENGLAND, UK

OWNERS Marc Newson & Charlotte Stockdale **OCCUPATION** Industrial designer & Stylist
PROPERTY Apartment, 390 sqm/4,200 sq ft gross floor; 2 floors; 7 rooms; 4 bathrooms
YEAR Building: 1894, Remodelling: 2009 **EXECUTIVE ARCHITECT** Squire and Partners,
London, www.squireandpartners.com **INTERIOR DESIGNERS** Marc Newson,
Sébastien Segers, architect, www.marc-newson.com, www.sebastiensegers.com
PHOTOGRAPHER Hugh Burden, www.hughburden.com

The flat is an Edwardian former mail sorting depot. Not wanting a loft, the owners took their inspiration from the style of the Frank Lloyd Wright house in "North By Northwest" and chalets. The result is warmth and originality.
Die Wohnung befindet sich in einer ehemaligen edwardianischen Postsortierstelle. Da die Besitzer kein Loft wollten, ließen sie sich von dem Haus im Stil von Frank Lloyd Wright aus dem Film „Der unsichtbare Dritte" inspirieren. Das Ergebnis ist ein Interior voller Wärme und Originalität.
L'appartement est situé dans un ancien centre de triage du début du 20ᵉ siècle. Ne souhaitant pas un loft (« ils sont grands et froids »), les propriétaires se sont inspirés de la maison du film « La Mort aux trousses » et des chalets de Frank Lloyd Wright.

P. 292 The Newson-designed "Voronoi Shelf," a sculptural work extracted from a single piece of marble. The skull is by Dustin Yellin. • Eines von Newson designtes „Voronoi"-Regal, das aus einem einzigen Marmorblock gefertigt wurde. Der Schädel ist von Dustin Yellin. • Des étagères « Voronoï » dessinées par Newson et taillées dans un seul bloc de marbre. Le crâne est une œuvre de Dustin Yellin.

P. 293 The kitchen and dining area features a number of Newson designs. Among them, the grey "Coast Chairs" and the "Dish Doctor" rack, both edited by Magis. He created the oven and hob for Smeg. • In der Küche und im Essbereich finden sich zahlreiche Newson-Designs, wie zum Beispiel die grauen

„Coast Chairs" und der Geschirrständer „Dish Doctor" (beide für Magis). Den Ofen und das Kochfeld entwarf er für Smeg. • Le coin cuisine et repas intègre de nombreuses pièces conçues par Newson. Parmi elles, les « Coast Chairs » grises et l'égouttoir « Dish Doctor », tous deux édités par Magis. Il a également dessiné le four et la hotte pour Smeg.

PP. 294–295 Newson has a particular liking for Celadon green and even had his Aston Martin DB4 painted that colour. Here, he chose it for the cupboards in the master bedroom. • Newson war schon immer von Blassgrün fasziniert und ließ sogar seinen Aston Martin DB4 in dieser Farbe spritzen. Auch die Schränke im Schlafzimmer

sind in diesem Farbton gehalten. • Newson a toujours eu une passion pour le vert pâle. Même son Aston Martin DB4 est peinte de cette couleur. Il l'a également choisie pour les placards de la chambre principale.

↖ A view into Newson and Stockdale's daughter Imogen's bathroom. • Blick in das Bad von Imogen, der Tochter von Stockdale und Newson. • Une vue de la salle de bain d'Imogen, la fille de Stockdale et de Newson.

→ The central staircase leads up into the library. • Die zentrale Treppe führt hinauf in die Bibliothek. • L'escalier central mène à la bibliothèque.

PP. 298–299 Newson searched for a month to find the rocks for the living room wall. They come from Nova Scotia. A Josef Frank fabric covers the Svenskt Tenn sofas. • Newson suchte lange, bis er die passenden Steine für die Wohnzimmerwand fand. Die Sofas von Svenskt Tenn sind mit einem Stoff von Josef Frank bezogen. • Newson a fait des recherches sur Internet pour trouver les galets du mur du séjour. Ils viennent de Nouvelle-Ecosse. Les canapés Svenskt Tenn sont tapissés d'un tissu de Josef Frank.

← The sofas are upholstered in tweed. • Die Sofas sind mit einem Tweedstoff bezogen. • Les canapés sont tapissés en tweed.

→ The oak panelling comes from a salvage company. • Die Eichentäfelung wurde bei einem Recyclingunternehmen für historische Baustoffe gekauft. • Les boiseries en chêne viennent d'une entreprise de récupération.

PP. 302–303 The Carrara marble bathroom is Newson's favourite room. The tub is from Drummonds. • Das mit Carrara-Marmor verkleidete Bad ist Newsons Lieblingsraum. Die Badewanne kommt von Drummonds. • La salle de bain, pièce préférée de Newson, est en marbre de Carrare. La baignoire vient de chez Drummonds.

"In Australia, where I grew up,
I never lived in a house with a library."

„In Australien, wo ich meine Kindheit verbrachte,
lebte ich nie in einem Haus mit Bibliothek."
« En Australie où j'ai grandi, je n'ai jamais vécu
dans une maison abritant une bibliothèque. »

LOS ANGELES
BEVERLY HILLS, USA

OWNER Eugenio López Alonso **OCCUPATION** Industrialist
PROPERTY House 697 sqm/7,500 sq ft gross floor; 1 floor; 12 rooms; 4.5 bathrooms
YEAR Building: 1957, Remodelling: 2003 **ARCHITECT** Original building: Wayne McAllister,
Remodelling: Ron Radziner, Marmol Radziner + Associates, www.marmol-radziner.com
Pool cabana: Steven Shortridge & David Spinelli, Shortridge Architects, www.callasarchitects.com
INTERIOR DESIGNERS Vance Burke & Todd Peter Vance Burke Design
PHOTOGRAPHER Tim Street-Porter, www.timstreetporter.com

The owner's aim was to respect the style and maintain the integrity of this mid-century gem. Original materials were kept or enhanced, and furniture added in neutral tones. The result, asserts López Alonso, is "clean, Californian, and very fresh."
Der Besitzer legte größten Wert darauf, die Integrität des Bauwerks aus den 1950ern zu bewahren. Er benutzte vorhandene Materialien und ergänzte sie mit Möbeln in neutralen Tönen. Das Ergebnis, so López Alonso, ist „klar, kalifornisch und sehr frisch".
L'objectif du propriétaire était de respecter le style et l'intégrité de ce bijou des années 1950. Les matériaux d'origine ont été mis en valeur. L'imposant mobilier reste dans les tons neutres. López Alonso est ravi du résultat qu'il trouve « net, californien et très frais ».

P. 304 Located up in the hills of Los Angeles, the 1957 structure features Palos Verdes stone and strong horizontal lines. • Das 1957 in den Bergen von Los Angeles gebaute Haus (errichtet mit Steinen aus Palos Verdes) zeichnet sich durch kraftvolle horizontale Linien aus. • Les pierres sèches de Palos Verdes et les lignes horizontales donnent tout son caractère à cette villa construite en 1957 sur les hauteurs de Los Angeles.

P. 305 Behind the pool stands a Jeff Koons' yellow "Elephant" sculpture in high chromium stainless steel. • Hinter dem Pool steht ein gelber „Elephant" von Jeff Koons aus verchromtem Edelstahl. • Derrière la piscine, une sculpture jaune « Elephant » de Jeff Koons en inox chromé.

PP. 306-307 The swimming pool was part of the original house. The circular sofa beside it was created by designers Vance Burke and Todd Peter. • Der Swimmingpool gehörte bereits zum ursprünglichen Entwurf. Das kreisrunde Sofa am Poolrand ist ein Entwurf der Designer Vance Burke und Todd Peter. • La piscine a été construite en même temps que la maison. Le canapé rond au bord de l'eau a été créé par les designers Vance Burke et Todd Peter.

The sofa in the living room was inspired by an Isamu Noguchi design of the 1940s. The white arm chair is only one of three surviving examples of a model created by a disciple of Carlo Mollino – Carlo Graffi. • Das Sofa im Wohnzimmer entstand nach einem Design von Isamu Noguchi aus den 1940ern. Der weiße Sessel ist eines von nur drei noch erhaltenen Exem-

plaren eines Modells, das Carlo Graffi, ein Schüler von Carlo Mollino, designt hat. • Dans le séjour, le canapé a été inspiré par un design d'Isamu Noguchi des années 1940. Le fauteuil blanc est l'un des trois derniers exemplaires d'un modèle créé par Carlo Graffi, un disciple de Carlo Mollino.

↑ Maurizio Cattelan's "Love Lasts Forever." • Maurizio Cattelans „Love Lasts Forever". • « Love Lasts Forever » de Maurizio Cattelan.

"When I saw the house for the first time,
  I knew it was for me."

„Als ich das Haus zum ersten Mal sah,
  wusste ich, dass es wie für mich gemacht war."
« Quand j'ai vu la maison pour la première fois,
  j'ai su qu'elle était pour moi. »

↖ A Claes Oldenburg sculpture stands behind a Vladimir Kagan sofa and a George Nakashima table in the master bedroom. • Im Hauptschlafzimmer: eine Skulptur von Claes Oldenburg hinter einem Sofa von Vladimir Kagan und einem Tisch von George Nakashima. • Dans la chambre principale, une sculpture de Claes Oldenburg se dresse derrière un canapé de Vladimir Kagan et une table basse de George Nakashima.

↑ The artwork behind the master bed is a 1973 Ed Ruscha oil painting entitled "Virtue." • Bei dem Kunstwerk über dem Bett handelt es sich um ein Ölbild von Ed Ruscha mit dem Titel „Virtue" aus dem Jahr 1973. • Au-dessus du lit de la chambre principale, une peinture à l'huile d'Ed Ruscha datant de 1973 et intitulée « Virtue ».

PP. 314–315 The library is decorated with a Jean Royère sofa, a Carlo Scarpa chair and a George Nakashima table. • Die Bibliothek ist mit einem Sofa von Jean Royère, einem Sessel von Carlo Scarpa und einem Tisch von George Nakashima eingerichtet. • Dans la bibliothèque, un canapé de Jean Royère, un fauteuil de Carlo Scarpa et une table basse de George Nakashima.

← The tub provides a spectacular view over the swimming pool. • Die Badewanne bietet einen fantastischen Blick auf den Swimmingpool. • De la baignoire, on a une vue spectaculaire sur la piscine.

↑ The master bathroom features a terrazzo vanity and a Palos Verdes stone wall. • Im Badezimmer sieht man einen Waschtisch aus Terrazzo und eine Wand aus Palos-Verdes-Steinen. • Le mur en pierres sèches de Palos Verdes dans la salle de bain principale contraste avec la sous-vasque en terrazzo.

PP. 318–319 Jack Pierson's "Night." • „Night" von Jack Pierson. • Des enseignes « Night » de Jack Pierson.

317

MADRID
EL VISO, SPAIN

OWNER Oliva García-Velarde **OCCUPATION** Interior designer
PROPERTY House, 240 sqm/2,600 sq ft gross floor; 3 floors; 4 rooms;
4 bathrooms **YEAR** Building: 1940, Remodelling: 2005 **INTERIOR**
DESIGNER Oliva García-Velarde/OGVA Interior **PHOTOGRAPHER** Pablo
Gómez Zuloaga **PHOTO STYLIST** Inés Sentmenat

The owner calls her style a "new minimalism" and provides warmth by playing with textures and references to the past. Art is another prerequisite. As she says, "It gives another dimension to our homes."
Die Besitzerin bezeichnet ihren Stil als „neuen Minimalismus" und verleiht ihren Räumen Wärme, indem sie mit Strukturen und Verweisen auf die Vergangenheit spielt. „Dadurch erhält unser Zuhause eine neue Dimension."
La propriétaire qualifie son style de « nouveau minimalisme » et a créé une atmosphère chaleureuse en jouant avec les textures et les références au passé. La présence de l'art est également indispensable. Comme elle l'explique : « Il apporte une autre dimension à nos maisons ».

P. 320 A view from the office into the library. A "Luxo L-1" lamp by Jac Jacobsen stands on a desk of García-Velarde's own design. The chairs were created by Charles and Ray Eames. • Blick vom Büro in die Bibliothek. Eine „Luxo L-1"-Lampe von Jac Jacobsen auf einem Tisch von García-Velarde. Die Stühle sind von Charles und Ray Eames. • Vue de la bibliothèque depuis le bureau. Une lampe « Luxo L-1 » de Jac Jacobsen sur une table de travail dessi-née par García-Velarde. Les chaises ont été créées par les Eames.

P. 321 On the office wall is a light box by Ignacio Llamas. The marble sculpture in the foreground is the work of Juan Asensio. • An der Wand im Büro hängt ein Lichtkasten von Ignacio Llamas. Die Marmorskulptur im Vordergrund ist eine Arbeit von Juan Asensio. • Une boîte lumineuse d'Ignacio Llamas orne un des murs du bureau. La sculpture en marbre au premier plan est de Juan Asensio.

← ↑ A "Panton" chair and 18th-century Piedmont chairs surround an Eero Saarinen "Tulip" table in the informal dining room; above them hangs an antique painted-iron chande-lier. • Ein „Panton"-Stuhl und Stühle aus dem Piemont um einen „Tulip"-Tisch von Eero Saarinen im informellen Ess-zimmer; darüber hängt ein antiker Kron-leuchter aus matt lackiertem Eisen. • Une chaise « Panton » et des fauteuils piémontais du 18ᵉ siècle entourent une table « Tulip » d'Eero Saarinen ; au-dessus de celle-ci, un lustre ancien en fer forgé peint.

↑ A steel sculpture by Blanca Muñoz and an 18th-century gilded bergère in one of the bedrooms. • Eine Stahl-skulptur von Blanca Muñoz in einem der Schlafzimmer. • Dans une chambre, une sculpture en acier de Blanca Muñoz et une bergère en bois doré du 18ᵉ siècle.

→ A 1960s American chair stands on a zebra rug in the library. Near the door are two 1950s Swedish prototype lamps. • Ein Stuhl aus den 1960ern in der Bib-liothek. Neben der Tür zum Büro stehen zwei schwedische Prototyp-Lampen aus den 1950ern. • Dans la biblithèque, un siège américain des années 1960. Près de la porte du bureau, deux prototypes de luminaires suédois des années 1950.

MARRAKECH
MOROCCO

OWNERS Emma Rochlitzer & Roberto Caciolli **OCCUPATION** Entrepreneur
PROPERTY Riad, 750 sqm/8,070 sq ft gross floor; 3 floors; 14 rooms;
7 bathrooms **YEAR** Building: early 19th century, Remodelling: 2004
ARCHITECTS Alessandra Lippini & Fabrizio Bizzarri, Ministero del Gusto,
www.ministerodelgusto.com **INTERIOR DESIGNERS** Emma Rochlitzer & Roberto Caciolli
PHOTOGRAPHER Giorgio Possenti/VegaMG, www.vegamg.it

The restoration of this riad highlighted its unusual verticality, emphasised by the columns of the patio. Reflecting the owners' European roots, the furnishings are largely design pieces from the 1950s to 1970s.

Bei der Restaurierung dieses alten Riads wurde die Vertikalität des Hauses unterstrichen, die durch die Säulen im Innenhof zusätzlich betont wird. Die Einrichtung besteht weitgehend aus Designobjekten der 1950er bis 1970er und reflektiert die europäischen Wurzeln der Besitzer.

Un riad restauré en mettant l'accent sur sa verticalité que soulignent les colonnes du patio. L'ameublement, composé en grande partie de meubles design des années 1950 à 1970, reflète les racines européennes des propriétaires.

P. 326 A collection of vintage radios from the 1930s to 1950s found at the Marrakech flea market creates a totem-like sculpture against the tadelakt wall. • Vor einer mit Tadelakt verputzten Wand sind alte Radios aus den 1930er- bis 1950er-Jahren zu einer totemartigen Skulptur angeordnet. • Une collection de radios des années 1930 à 1950 crée une sculpture totem devant un mur en tadelakt.

P. 327 Marrakech's oldest and largest mosque, the Koutoubia, at sunset. • Die Koutoubia, die älteste und größte Moschee von Marrakesch, bei Sonnenuntergang. • La mosquée Koutoubia, la plus ancienne et la plus grande de Marrakech, au coucher du soleil.

PP. 328–329 A Joe Colombo "Elda" armchair and vintage "Sacco" pouf from Zanotta on the main patio; "Mouchara-

bieh" panels were added to the windows and balconies. • Ein „Elda"-Sessel von Joe Colombo und ein „Sacco"-Sitzsack von Zanotta im Innenhof; Fenster und Balkone wurden mit „Moucharabieh", ornamentalen Eisengittern, versehen. • Dans le patio principal, un fauteuil « Elda » de Joe Colombo et un vieux pouf « Sacco » de chez Zanotta ; des moucharabiehs ont été ajoutés aux fenêtres et aux balcons.

← Under the main stairs, French 1950s vases and candle holders on a 1970s steel and wood table. • Unter der Haupttreppe: französische Vasen und Kerzenleuchter aus den 1950ern auf einem Tisch aus Stahl und Holz aus den 1970ern. • Sous l'escalier principal, des vases et des bougeoirs français des années 1950 sur un guéridon en bois et acier des années 1970.

↑ The Moroccan living room is furnished with chairs and a plastic coffee table from the Bab Lakmis flea market. • Das marokkanische Wohnzimmer ist mit Sesseln und einem Couchtisch aus Kunststoff eingerichtet, der vom Flohmarkt an der Bab Lakmis stammt. • Le salon marocain est meublé de fauteuils et d'une table basse en plastique chinés sur le marché aux puces Bab Lakmis.

PP. 332–333 A black 19th-century Murano mirror adorns one of the walls of the same room. • Ein schwarzer Murano-Spiegel aus dem 19. Jahrhundert ziert eine der Wände des Zimmers. • Un miroir noir de Murano du 19e siècle orne un des murs du salon.

← The tub in the master bathroom is made from white tadelakt. The early 20th-century Murano mirror was bought in Venice. • Die Wanne im Hauptbadezimmer ist aus weißem Tadelakt gefertigt. Der Murano-Spiegel aus dem frühen 20. Jahrhundert wurde in Venedig gekauft. • La baignoire dans la salle de bain principale est en tadelakt blanc. Le miroir de Murano du début du 20ᵉ siècle a été acheté à Venise.

→ A detail of the concrete washbasin in the master bathroom. • Detail des Beton-Waschbeckens im Hauptbadezimmer. • Détail du lavabo en béton dans la salle de bain principale.

P. 334 The geometric chevron pattern of the wall behind the bed was created using small bricks. The vintage bedspread, made from wool and sequins, is from the Atlas region. • Das geometrische Chevron-Muster der Wand hinter dem Bett wurde mit kleinen Klinkern gebildet. Die paillettenbesetzte Tagesdecke aus Wolle kommt aus der Atlas-Region. • Le motif géométrique en chevrons du mur situé derrière le lit a été réalisé avec de petites briques. Le dessus-de-lit ancien, en laine et sequins, vient de la région de l'Atlas.

P. 335 The enormous 18th-century Venetian crystal chandelier is one of 13 the owners bought in Cairo at the auction of an ancient sultan's palace. Under the table is an old Touareg carpet made from camel leather. • Der enorme venezianische Kristalllüster aus dem 18. Jahrhundert ist eines von 13 Exemplaren, die die Besitzer bei einer Auktion in Kairo erwarben, in der das Inventar eines alten Sultanspalastes versteigert wurde. Unter dem Tisch liegt ein Tuareg-Teppich aus Kamelleder. • L'énorme lustre vénitien en cristal du 18ᵉ siècle fait partie des treize que les propriétaires ont achetés au Caire lors de la vente aux enchères d'un ancien palais du sultan. Sous la table, un tapis touareg ancien en peau de chameau.

MELBOURNE
VICTORIA, AUSTRALIA

OWNER David Bromley **OCCUPATION** Artist **PROPERTY** Apartment
1,350 sqm/14,500 sq ft gross floor; 2 floors; 16 rooms; 3 bathrooms
YEAR Building: 1890, Remodelling: 2006 **ARCHITECT** George McMullen
PHOTOGRAPHER Jeremy Blincoe, www.jeremyblincoe.com

Owner David Bromley has always loved "environments that envelop you in their stories and emotions." His apartment in an old Victorian shopping arcade retains its aged effect, with eccentric and intriguing objects.
David Bromley war schon immer „verliebt in Interiors, die dich mit ihren Geschichten und Emotionen umfangen". Seine Wohnung in einer alten viktorianischen Einkaufspassage hat sich ihre altmodische Ausstrahlung bewahrt.
Le propriétaire, David Bromley, est « amoureux des environnements qui vous enveloppent avec leurs histoires et leurs émotions ». Son appartement situé dans une ancienne galerie marchande victorienne a conservé toute sa patine. Les objets y sont excentriques et intrigants.

P. 338 The window coverings in the study are made from vintage kabuki screens. On the table are a "Bells" advertising sign, French skittles and Indian wooden horses. • Die Rollos an den Fenstern sind aus alten Kabuki-Wandschirmen gefertigt. Auf dem Tisch stehen eine Reklametafel von „Bells", französische Kegel und indische Holzpferde. • Les stores dans l'atelier sont réalisés avec d'anciens paravents de Kabuki. Sur la table, un panneau publicitaire « Bells », un jeu de quilles français et des chevaux de bois indiens.

P. 339 A view of the stairs from the main entrance. The chandelier is Argentinian. In the foreground are a French concrete bird bath and a bronze sculpture created by Bromley. • Blick vom Haupteingang zur Treppe. Der Kronleuchter kommt aus Argentinien. Im Vordergrund stehen ein französisches Vogelbad aus Beton und eine Bronzeskulptur von Bromley. • Une vue de l'escalier depuis l'entrée. Le lustre est argentin. Au premier plan, une vasque pour oiseaux française en béton et une sculpture en bronze réalisée par Bromley.

PP. 340–341 In the living-dining room: chairs sourced locally around a Danish table, acrylic and metal leaf butterfly paintings by Bromley. • Im Wohn- und Esszimmer: Stühle aus der Region um einen dänischen Tisch. Die Gemälde sind von Bromley. • Dans le séjour et la salle à manger, des chaises de la région autour d'une table danoise. Les tableaux sont de Bromley.

← A bronze Bromley sculpture in the gallery. • Eine Bronzeskulptur von Bromley in der Galerie. • Dans la galerie, une sculpture en bronze de Bromley.

↓ Kilim cushions, an Australian harp and a "Milka" cow in a guest bedroom. • Kelimkissen, eine australische Harfe und eine „Milka"-Kuh im Gästezimmer. • Dans une chambre d'amis, des coussins en kilim, une harpe australienne et une vache « Milka ».

PP. 344–345 A Bromley sculpture and
a Spanish horse's head in the living room.
• Die Skulptur eines malenden Jungen
von Bromley und ein spanischer Pferde-
kopf im Wohnzimmer. • Dans le séjour,
une sculpture de Bromley et une tête de
cheval espagnole.

↑ On a patio, antique glass bottles are
arranged on a table. • Auf der Veranda:
antike Glasflaschen auf einem Tisch.
• Sur le balcon, des bonbonnes en verre
anciennes disposées sur une table.

↑ The studio with a Greek vase and old French chairs. • Eine griechische Bodenvase und alte französische Stühle im Atelier. • Dans l'atelier, un vase grec et des chaises anciennes françaises.

PP. 348–349 A French four-poster with suzanis and Bromley paintings in the master bedroom. • Im Hauptschlafzimmer: ein französisches Himmelbett mit einer Suzani-Tagesdecke und Gemälde von Bromley. • Un lit à baldaquin français et des tableaux peints par Bromley dans la chambre principale.

MEUDON
ÎLE-DE-FRANCE, FRANCE

OCCUPANT Alexis Lahellec **OCCUPATION** Galerist
PROPERTY House, 250 sqm/2,691 sq ft gross floor; 2 floors;
5 rooms; 2 bathrooms **YEAR** Building: 1953 **ARCHITECT** Claude Parent
PHOTOGRAPHER Ricardo Labougle, www.ricardolabougle.com
PHOTO PRODUCER Ana Cardinale, www.anacardinale.com

Built as an atelier for sculptor André Bloc, this Modernist house had been restructured in the 1980s. Lahellec recreated the original volumes, brought the red inside the house, and furnished it mainly with designs from the 1950s.
Ursprünglich als Atelier für den Bildhauer André Bloc errichtet, wurde dieses modernistische Haus in den 1980ern umgebaut. Lahellec stellte die frühere Raumaufteilung wieder her und stattete es hauptsächlich mit Designs der 1950er aus.
Construite pour servir d'atelier au sculpteur André Bloc, cette structure moderniste a été rénovée dans les années 1980. Lahellec a recréé les espaces d'origine, a fait entrer le rouge à l'intérieur de la maison et l'a aménagée principalement avec du mobilier design des années 1950.

P. 350   The cubic structure is almost hidden from view by the trees. • Bäume schirmen das kubische Gebäude von den Blicken der Passanten ab. • La structure cubique est presque entièrement cachée par les arbres.

P. 351   On the terrace, Mathieu Matégot's wrought-iron "Cap d'Ail" dining table and chairs cohabit with a marble sculpture by Bloc. • Auf der Terrasse stehen Mathieu Matégots schmiedeeiserner „Cap d'Ail"-Esstisch, Stühle und eine Marmorskulptur von Bloc in trauter Eintracht nebeneinander. • Sur la terrasse, une table et des chaises en fer forgé « Cap d'Ail » de Mathieu Matégot cohabitent avec une sculpture en marbre d'André Bloc.

P. 352–353   In the first-floor office, a "Revolt" chair by Friso Kramer stands at a 1950s desk. • Im Büro im oberen Stock steht ein „Revolt"-Stuhl von Friso Kramer an einem Schreibtisch aus den 1950ern. • Dans le bureau du premier étage, une chaise « Revolt » de Friso Kramer devant un secrétaire des années 1950.

← Surrounded by lush vegetation, the house completely turns its back to the street. The sculpture to the left of the pool is another work by Bloc. • Das von üppiger Vegetation umgebene Haus ist vollständig von der Straße abgewandt. Die Skulptur links vom Pool wurde ebenfalls von Bloc geschaffen. • Entourée d'une végétation luxuriante, la maison tourne le dos à la rue. A gauche de la piscine, une autre sculpture de Bloc.

↑ Occupant Alexis Lahellec runs a 20th-century design gallery in the centre of Paris. • Der Bewohner Alexis Lahellec führt eine Designgalerie mit Kunst des 20. Jahrhunderts im Zentrum von Paris. • L'habitant, Alexis Lahellec, dirige une galerie spécialisée dans le design du 20e siècle, au cœur de Paris.

"You feel like you're in another world there, totally surrounded by that enchanting garden."

„Man kommt sich hier vor wie in einer anderen Welt –
    mit einem Ausblick in den Garten, der das Haus vollständig umgibt."
« On se sent dans un autre monde, face à ce jardin qui vous entoure. »

PP. 356–357 The sitting room is decorated with a yellow leather sofa and chairs from the "Togo" collection created by Michel Ducaroy for Ligne Roset in 1973. • Das Wohnzimmer ist mit einem gelben Ledersofa und gelben Sesseln aus der „Togo"-Kollektion ausgestattet, die Michel Ducaroy 1973 für Ligne Roset entwarf. • Dans le salon, un canapé et des fauteuils en cuir jaune de la collection « Togo » créée par Michel Ducaroy en 1973 pour la Ligne Roset.

PP. 358–359 A carafe by David Belugou stands on a steel and marble dining table created by Claudine Chazel and Michael Prentice. The forms of the Serge Mouille wall light provide the perfect counterpoint to André Bloc's masterful stained-glass window. • Auf dem Esstisch aus Stahl und Marmor von Claudine Chazel und Michael Prentice steht eine Karaffe von David Belugou. Die Formen der Wandleuchte von Serge Mouille bieten den perfekten Kontrapunkt zu André Blocs meisterlichem

Buntglasfenster. • Sur une table de salle à manger en acier et marbre créée par Claudine Chazel et Michael Prentice, une carafe de David Belugou. Les formes de l'applique de Serge Mouille offrent un contrepoint parfait à l'impressionnant vitrail d'André Bloc.

↖ → The kitchen has stainless steel units and white ceramic tiles. • Elemente aus Edelstahl und weiße Keramikfliesen in der Küche. • Dans la cuisine, des placards en inox et du carrelage en céramique blanc.

PP. 362–363 The living room features a red fireplace, an early 20th-century green Swedish armchair, an Alvar Aalto chaise longue and a spiral staircase. • Im Wohnzimmer stößt man auf einen roten Kamin, einen grünen schwedischen Sessel aus dem frühen 20. Jahrhundert, eine Alvar-Aalto-Chaiselongue und eine Wendeltreppe. • Dans le séjour, une cheminée rouge, un fauteuil

suédois du début du 20ᵉ siècle, une chaise longue d'Alvar Aalto et un escalier en colimaçon.

↑ A guestroom on the first floor offers spectacular views of the garden. • Das Gästezimmer im ersten Stock bietet einen fantastischen Blick auf den Garten. • Une chambre d'amis à l'étage jouit d'une vue spectaculaire sur le jardin.

→ The features in the guest shower room were added in the 1980s. Only the window is original to the house. • Das Gästebad wurde in den 1980ern umgestaltet. Nur das Fenster blieb unverändert. • Les éléments de cette salle d'eau des invités ont été ajoutés dans les années 1980. Seule la fenêtre est d'époque.

← Two paintings by the Portuguese-born artist Ernesto dominate the master bedroom. The bed linen is from Mia Zia. • Zwei Gemälde des in Portugal geborenen Malers Ernesto dominieren das große Schlafzimmer. Die Bettwäsche ist ein Design von Mia Zia. • Deux toiles du peintre Ernesto, né au Portugal, dominent la chambre principale. La literie vient de chez Mia Zia.

↑ Two red leather "AX" chairs designed in 1947 by Peter Hvidt and Orla Mølgaard Nielsen occupy one corner of the same room. The private terrace leads onto the garage roof. • In einer Ecke desselben Zimmers stehen zwei rote „AX"-Ledersessel, die 1947 von Peter Hvidt und Orla Mølgaard Nielsen designt wurden. Die kleine Terrasse führt auf das Dach der Garage. •

Dans un coin de la même chambre, deux fauteuil « AX » en cuir rouge conçus en 1947 par Peter Hvidt et Orla Mølgaard Nielsen. Le toit du garage a été converti en terrasse privée.

"Finding this house was like a dream.
Its architecture and history move me."

„Die Entdeckung dieses Haus war für mich wie ein Traum.
Seine Architektur und seine Geschichte berühren mich."
« Découvrir cette maison a été comme un rêve,
son architecture et son histoire me touchent. »

MIAMI
MIAMI SHORES, FLORIDA, USA

OWNER Doug Meyer **OCCUPATION** Designer
PROPERTY House, 210 sqm/2,300 sq ft gross floor; 1 floor;
8 rooms; 3 bathrooms **YEAR** Building: 1934, Remodelling: 2008
INTERIOR DESIGNERS Doug Meyer, Doug & Gene Meyer Studio, New York & Miami,
www.dougandgenemeyer.com **PHOTOGRAPHER** Arturo Zavala Haag/
Courtesy of AD Spain **PHOTO STYLIST** Doug Meyer

Doug Meyer's style influences include Louise Nevelson, David Hicks and Josef Albers. He describes his own home as "unexpected" and favours furniture and objects that take on a sculptural appearance, as well as striking, unusual colour schemes.

Der Stil von Doug Meyer ist vor allem von Louise Nevelson, David Hicks und Josef Albers beeinflusst. Er bevorzugt skulptural wirkende Möbel und Objekte sowie auffällige, ungewöhnliche Farbzusammenstellungen.

Doug Meyer a surtout été influencé par Louise Nevelson, David Hicks et Josef Albers. Qualifiant sa propre demeure « d'inattendue », il a un faible pour les meubles et les objets sculpturaux ainsi que pour les combinaisons de couleurs inhabituelles.

P. 368 The upper deck was painted to match the infinity pool, while the black and white striped awning was meant to evoke an "Old Miami Beach" mood. • Die obere Sonnenterrasse wurde passend zum Infinity Pool gestrichen, während die schwarz-weiß gestreifte Markise an das „klassische Miami Beach" erinnern soll. • La terrasse a été peinte de la même couleur que la piscine à débordement tandis que les auvents à rayures noires et blanches évoquent « le Miami d'antan ».

P. 369 Bright hues set the tone on the backyard lanai. The tower cubes are vintage 1970s Albrizzi. The Moroccan floor mat was purchased in Tangiers. • Auf der Veranda hinter dem Haus dominieren kräftige Farben. Die aufgetürmten Würfel aus den 1970ern stammen von Albrizzi; die marokkanische

Bodenmatte entdeckte Meyer in Tanger. • Des couleurs éclatantes donnent le ton sur la véranda à l'arrière de la maison. Les cubes empilés sont une édition des années 1970 d'Albrizzi. Le tapis marocain a été acheté à Tanger.

PP. 370–373 Loungers from the 1970s are shaded by a Thai umbrella; a 1960s set of furniture was coated lime green; Wendell Castle chairs on the upper deck. • Liegestühle aus den 1970ern unter einem thailändischen Sonnenschirm. Sessel von Wendell Castle auf der oberen Terrasse. • Sous un parasol traditionnel thaïlandais, deux chaises longues des années 1970 ; des meubles de jardin des années 1960 peints par poudrage en vert acidulé ; sur la terrasse supérieure, des sièges de Wendell Castle.

↑ The lounge features a Florence Knoll sofa, Martin Eisler and Carlo Hauner chairs and a Doug & Gene Meyer rug. • Die Lounge mit einem Sofa von Florence Knoll, Sesseln von Martin Eisler und Carlo Hauner sowie einem Teppich von Doug & Gene Meyer. • Dans le salon, un canapé de Florence Knoll, des fauteuils de Martin Eisler et de Carlo Hauner sur un tapis de Doug et Gene Meyer.

→ Louis XV chairs surround an Eero Saarinen table in the dining room. The photo of Ringo Starr is by Richard Avedon. • Im Esszimmer: Stühle im Louis-XV-Stil um einen Tisch von Eero Saarinen. Das Foto von Ringo Starr stammt von Richard Avedon. • Dans la salle à manger, des chaises « Louis XV » autour d'une table d'Eero Saarinen. Le portrait de Ringo Starr est de Richard Avedon.

PP. 376-377 In the living room, white Wendell Castle "Molar" chairs face a Milo Baughman sofa. • Im Wohnzimmer: weiße „Molar"-Sessel von Wendell Castle und ein Sofa von Milo Baughman. • Dans le séjour, des sièges « Molar » de Wendell Castle face à un canapé de Milo Baughman.

↑ An Italian ceramic head from the 1970s sits on a limestone mantel. • Ein Keramikkopf aus den 1970ern auf dem Kaminsims. • Une tête en céramique italienne des années 1970 sur un manteau de cheminée en liais.

→ The master bedroom has a pair of side tables created by Meyer. • Im Hauptschlafzimmer stehen einige von Meyer entworfene Beistelltische. • Dans la chambre principale, une paire de tables de nuit dessinées par Meyer.

PP. 380-381 One wall of the master bedroom has been covered in a collage of blue images. The wall sculpture above the lavender chest is by Curtis Jere. • Eine der Wände des Schlafzimmers ist mit einer Collage aus blauen Bildern bedeckt. Die Wandskulptur über der lilafarbenen Kommode stammt von Curtis Jere. • Un mur de la chambre principale a été tapissé d'un collage d'images bleues. La sculpture murale au-dessus de la commode mauve est de Curtis Jere.

378

← Above an orange lacquered cabinet in the dining room, Meyer created a wall sculpture using mirror and Lucite panels. • Über einem orangefarben lackierten Schrank im Esszimmer hängt eine Wandskulptur, die Meyer aus Spiegel- und Lucite-Plättchen angefertigt hat. • Dans la salle à manger, au-dessus d'un cabinet laqué orange, Meyer a créé une sculpture murale avec un miroir et des panneaux en Lucite.

↑ The designer on the front porch in front of a yellow and white mural he painted. • Der Designer auf der vorderen Veranda vor einem von ihm gemalten Wandbild in Gelb und Weiß. • Le designer, sur le porche orné d'une fresque jaune et blanche qu'il a peinte lui-même.

PP. 384–385 The artwork in the guest room is from Meyer's "BOD" series. • Das Kunstwerk im Gästezimmer gehört zu Meyers „BOD"-Serie. • Les œuvres accrochées dans la chambre d'amis appartiennent à la série « BOD » de Meyer.

MILAN
LOMBARDY, ITALY

OWNERS Britt Moran & Emiliano Salci **OCCUPATION** Designers
PROPERTY Apartment, 350 sqm/3,800 sq ft gross floor; 1 floor; 7 rooms;
2 bathrooms **YEAR** Building: 1750, Remodelling: 2008 **ARCHITECTS &
INTERIOR DESIGNERS** Britt Moran & Emiliano Salci, Dimore Studio,
www.dimorestudio.eu **PHOTOGRAPHER** Andrea Ferrari, www.andreaferrari.info

The aim was to be true to the space, accentuating its character and inserting objects from different periods. Deliberate contrasts provide a mix of theatricality and irony. Things stay simple "without being predictable."
Hier galt es, die Originalräume zu bewahren und deren besondere Merkmale sowie die eingebauten Möbel und Objekte aus verschiedenen Perioden und Stilepochen ins rechte Licht zu setzen. Durch bewusst gesetzte Kontraste entsteht eine Mischung aus Theatralität und Ironie.
L'objectif était de rester fidèle à l'espace tout en accentuant ses caractéristiques et en y intégrant des meubles et des objets de toutes les époques et styles. Les contrastes créent théâtralité et humour. Le décor reste simple « sans être prévisible ».

← A view of the hallway with its elaborate architectural detailing. • Blick in den Korridor mit seinen kunstvollen architektonischen Details. • Une vue du couloir avec ses détails architecturaux ouvragés.

→ In one of the bedrooms, reclaimed hotel sign letters stand atop a Dimore Studio wardrobe clad in painter's canvas. • In einem der Schlafzimmer: Buchstaben vom Schriftzug eines ehemaligen Hotels auf einem Kleiderschrank von Dimore Studio, der mit Leinwand bespannt ist. • Dans l'une deschambres, une ancienne enseigne d'hôtel posée sur une penderie de Dimore Studio tapissée en toile de peintre.

P. 386 In the living room, a 17th-century sofa, two Chiavarine armchairs, and a Touareg mat. • Im Wohnzimmer: ein antikes Sofa, zwei Chiavarine-Sessel und ein Tuareg-Teppich. • Dans le séjour, un canapé du 17ᵉ siècle, deux fauteuils Chiavarine et un tapis touareg.

P. 387 A Carlo Mollino armchair stands in front of a lacquered console created by Dimore Studio. Above it is a 17th-century frontispiece in silk and silver. • Ein Sessel von Carlo Mollino vor einer lackierten Konsole von Dimore Studio. • Un fauteuil de Carlo Mollino devant une console laquée créée par Dimore Studio. Au-dessus, une tapisserie du 17ᵉ siècle en soie et fil d'argent.

PP. 388–389 In the kitchen, a Verner Panton light above an Eero Saarinen table. A "Raffles" sofa by Vico Magistretti placed next to Achille Castiglioni's "Arco" floor lamp. • In der Küche hängt eine Leuchte von Verner Panton über einem Tisch von Eero Saarinen. Ein „Raffles"-Sofa von Vico Magistretti neben Achille Castiglionis „Arco"-Stehlampe. • Dans la cuisine, un plafonnier de Verner Panton au-dessus d'une table d'Eero Saarinen. Le lampadaire « Arco » d'Achille Castiglioni a trouvé sa place près d'un canapé « Raffles » de Vico Magistretti.

PP. 392–393 In the reception room, a decorative flower pot holder from the late 1800s stands on one of two 16th-century monastery tables from Lucca. On the wall is a rare Henri Coleman shelf. • Im Empfangszimmer steht ein dekorativer Übertopf aus dem späten 19. Jahrhundert auf einem von zwei Klostertischen aus dem 16. Jahrhundert aus Lucca. An der Wand hängt ein seltenes Regal von Henri Coleman. • Dans l'antichambre, une jardinière décorative de la fin du 19ᵉ siècle sur l'une des deux tables provenant d'un monastère du 16ᵉ siècle à Lucques. Au mur, une étagère rare d'Henri Coleman.

NEW YORK

USA

OWNER Izhar Patkin **OCCUPATION** Artist
PROPERTY Loft **YEAR** Building: late 19th century,
Remodelling: 1995 **PHOTOGRAPHER** François Halard/TASCHEN,
www.francoishalard.com

A home and studio in part of an old schoolhouse. Intervention was largely limited to creating courtyards to bring in light and air. Eclectic furnishings "by people whose imagination and creativity I respect."

Eine Wohnung mit Atelier in einem Trakt einer ehemaligen alten Schule. Der Eingriff beschränkte sich weitgehend auf die Anlage von Innenhöfen. Die Einrichtungsstücke sind eklektisch. „Sie wurden von Menschen geschaffen, deren Fantasie und Kreativität ich wirklich respektiere."

Une maison et un atelier créés dans une partie d'une ancienne école. Le mobilier est éclectique mais significatif. « Ce sont des pièces réalisées par des personnes dont je respecte l'imagination et la créativité. »

P. 394 A number of artworks hang in the airy studio space. On the far wall is a 2006 piece entitled "Arik Patkin WTC," created with ink on pleated tulle. • Im luftigen Atelierraum hängen zahlreiche Kunstwerke. Die Arbeit von 2006 an der hinteren Wand trägt den Titel „Arik Patkin WTC" und wurde mit Tinte auf plissiertem Tüll gefertigt. • Plusieurs œuvres d'art sont accrochées dans l'atelier lumineux. Sur le mur du fond, une œuvre de 2006 intitulée « Arik Patkin WTC » réalisée à l'encre sur du tulle plissé.

P. 395 In one of the courtyards, blossoms fall onto Harry Bertoia chairs and Moroccan tray tables. • In einem der Höfe fallen Blüten auf Stühle von Harry Bertoia und auf Tische aus marokkanischen Tabletts. • Dans l'une des cours, une pluie de fleurs tombe sur des chaises d'Harry Bertoia et des tables à plateau marocaines.

P. 396 The artist also created the main entrance door using coloured blown glass. • Der Künstler schuf auch die Tür des Haupteingangs, für die er mundgeblasenes Buntglas verwendete. • L'artiste a également réalisé la porte d'entrée avec du verre de couleur soufflé.

P. 397 Artist Kim MacConnel handpainted both the chairs and curtain. The torch in the corner was made from plastic Indian lanterns. • Der Künstler Kim MacConnel hat die Sessel und den Vorhang von Hand bemalt. Bei der Stehlampe dienen indische Laternen als Lampenschirme. • L'artiste Kim MacConnel a peint les fauteuils et le rideau. La torchère a été réalisée avec des lampes indiennes en plastique.

↑ Patkin's kitchen chandelier comprises both decorative and functional glassware. • Patkins Kronleuchter in der Küche ist dekorativ und funktional zugleich. • Pour sa cuisine, Patkin a créé un lustre avec des verres décoratifs et fonctionnels.

← Sikh wedding scarves act as curtains in the dressing room. The lantern once hung in a Lower East Side synagogue. • Im Ankleidezimmer dienen Hochzeitsschals der Sikhs als Vorhänge. Die Laterne hing einst in einer Synagoge auf der Lower East Side. • Dans le dressing, des étoles de mariage sikhes servent de rideaux. La lanterne vient d'une synagogue du Lower East Side.

→ Izhar Patkin in front of one of his own creations – a 1987 ink on pleated neoprene piece called "Holly's Dining." The chair was painted by Kim MacConnel. • Besitzer Izhar Patkin vor einer seiner eigenen Kreationen, einer aus Tinte auf plissiertem Neopren bestehenden Arbeit von 1987 mit dem Titel „Holly's Dining". Der Sessel wurde von Kim MacConnel bemalt. • Le propriétaire Izhar Patkin devant l'une de ses créations : une œuvre à l'encre sur une feuille de néoprène plissée datant de 1987 et intitulée « Holly's Dining ». Le fauteuil a été peint par MacConnel.

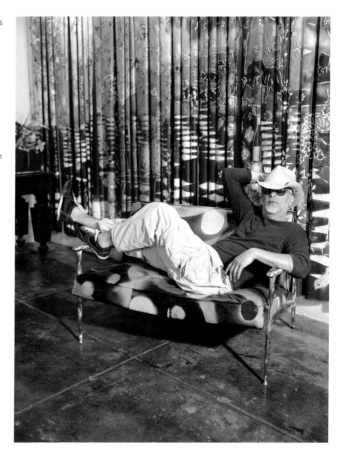

P. 399 In the meeting room, old school chairs surround a table made by placing a plywood top onto saw-horses. The mural on wood was inspired by Pennsylvania-Dutch barn paintings and Kafka's parable "Before the Law." • Im Besprechungszimmer stehen alte Schulstühle um einen Tisch, der aus einer Sperrholzplatte auf Sägeböcken besteht. Das auf Holz gemalte Bild an der hinteren Wand ist von den Scheunenbildern der Pennsylvania Dutch sowie von Kafkas Parabel „Vor dem Gesetz" inspiriert. • Dans la salle de réunion, de vieilles chaises d'école entourent une table constituée d'une planche de contreplaqué posée sur des tréteaux. L'œuvre sur bois occupant tout un mur s'inspire des peintures réalisées par les Hollandais de Pennsylvanie sur leurs granges et de la parabole de Kafka « Devant la loi ».

PP. 402–403 In the living room, more MacConnel pieces and a Patkin artwork based on photos of his parents' wedding. • Im Wohnzimmer sind weitere Arbeiten von MacConnel zu sehen sowie ein Werk von Patkin, das auf Hochzeitsfotos seiner Eltern basiert. • Dans le séjour, des créations de MacConnel et une œuvre de Patkin basée sur des photos du mariage de ses parents.

NEW YORK

NOHO, USA

OWNERS Tomoko & Kimio Akiyoshi **OCCUPATION** Visual merchandiser & Salon owner
PROPERTY Loft, 120 sqm/1,300 sq ft gross floor; 1.5 floors; 5 rooms; 2 bathrooms
YEAR Building: 1900, Remodelling: 2008 **ARCHITECTS & INTERIOR DESIGNERS**
Mishi Hosono & Adam Weintraub, Koko Architecture + Design, New York,
www.kokoarch.com **PHOTOGRAPHER** Trevor Tondro, www.trevortondro.com

A design that combines "the simplicity of Japanese interiors with the optimism of postwar modernism." Based on the "bento box," it offers clever storage solutions and space that is extended vertically.
Ein Design, das „die Schlichtheit japanischer Einrichtungen mit dem Optimismus der Nachkriegsmoderne kombiniert". Basierend auf der „Bentobox", bietet der Entwurf clevere Aufbewahrungslösungen und vertikal ausgedehnte Räume.
Une esthétique qui conjugue « la simplicité des intérieurs japonais et l'optimisme du modernisme d'après-guerre ». S'inspirant du « bento box », l'agencement inclut des rangements astucieux et un espace qui s'étend verticalement.

P. 404 Tomoko and Kimio Akiyoshi
with their daughters Sora (left) and Umi
at the kitchen counter. The barstools are
the "Hi-Pad" model designed by Jasper
Morrison for Cappellini. • Tomoko und
Kimio Akiyoshi mit ihren Töchtern Sora
(links) und Umi an der Küchentheke.
Bei den Hockern handelt es sich um das
Modell „Hi-Pad" von Jasper Morrison für
Cappellini. • Tomoko et Kimio Akiyoshi
avec leurs filles Sora (à gauche) et Umi
autour du comptoir de la cuisine. Les
tabourets « Hi-Pad » ont été dessinés
par Jasper Morrison pour Cappellini.

P. 405 In the living room, a George
Nelson "Case Study" couch and Jon

Gasca nesting tables. The stairs lead up
to Kimio Akiyoshi's photo lab. • Eine
Couch aus der Case-Study-Reihe von
George Nelson und ein Satztisch von
Jon Gasca im Wohnzimmer. Die Treppe
führt hinauf in das Fotolabor von Kimio
Akiyoshi. • Dans le séjour, un canapé
« Case Study » de George Nelson et des
tables gigognes de Jon Gasca. L'escalier
mène au labo photo de Kimio Akiyoshi.

↑ Bright hues were used for the inside
of the kitchen cupboards. • Für die
Innenseiten der Küchenschränke
wurden leuchtende Farben gewählt.
• L'intérieur des placards de la cuisine
a été peint de couleurs vives.

→ Orange Eames chairs provide a
flash of colour. The dining table is the
"Melltorp" model created by Lisa
Norinder for IKEA. The pendant lights
above the counter are by Erik Møller.
• Orangefarbene Eames-Sessel sorgen
für einen farbigen Akzent. Bei dem
Esstisch handelt es sich um das Modell
„Melltorp", das Lisa Norinder für Ikea
entworfen hat. Die Hängeleuchte über
der Theke ist ein Design von Erik Møller.
• Les chaises orange des Eames offrent
une tache de couleur. La table « Melltorp »
a été créée par Lisa Norinder pour Ikea.
Les plafonniers au-dessus du comptoir
sont d'Erik Møller.

↑ Storage bins have been integrated into the platform of the master bedroom. • In das Podest des Hauptschlafzimmers wurden Aufbewahrungsboxen eingebaut. • Des casiers de rangement ont été intégrés sous l'estrade de la chambre principale.

↗ The bedroom is very white and serene. Frosted doors separate the space from the living area. • Das Schlafzimmer ist völlig weiß und sehr ruhig gehalten. Milchglastüren trennen den Raum vom Wohnbereich. • La chambre est toute blanche et sereine. Elle est séparée du séjour par des portes coulissantes en verre dépoli.

→ During the day, the foldable mattresses from Muji are stored under trap doors in the floor. • Tagsüber werden die zusammenklappbaren Matratzen von Muji unter den Falltüren im Boden verstaut. • Pendant la journée, les matelas pliants de chez Muji sont rangés sous des trappes dans l'estrade.

"Whenever I go into the bedroom, I feel rested."

„Immer wenn ich ins Schlafzimmer gehe, fühle ich mich ausgeruht."
« Chaque fois que j'entre dans la chambre, je me sens reposé. »

↑ The desk chair is from the Eames "Aluminium Group" and the holes in the wall are part of a unit for drying clothes. • Der Schreibtischstuhl ist Teil der „Aluminium Group" von Eames, und die Löcher in der Wand gehören zu einer Vorrichtung zum Trocknen von Wäsche. • Le fauteuil de bureau appartient à la série « Aluminium Group » des Eames et les trous dans la cloison font partie d'un espace sèche-linge.

→ Each of the girls has her own work station at the front of the bedroom. The storage units are faced with blue laminate and the red Eames fibreglass chair still has its original casters. • Jedes der Mädchen hat vorne im Schlafzimmer

seinen eigenen Schreibtisch. Die Hängeschränke sind mit blauem Folienlaminat beschichtet, und der rote Glasfaser-Sessel von Eames besitzt noch immer seine Originalrollen. • Chacune des filles a son propre bureau à l'avant de la chambre. Les armoires sont recouvertes de laminé bleu et la chaise rouge Eames possède encore ses roulettes d'origine.

P. 412 Among the objects Sora stores next to the steps of her bed are Sonny Angel dolls by Dreams and a glass Astro Boy statue from Kiddy Land Tokyo. • Zu den Objekten, die Sora neben der Leiter zu ihrem Bett aufbewahrt, gehören auch Sonny-Angel-Puppen von Dreams und eine gläserne Astro-Boy-Figur von Kiddy

Land Tokyo. • Parmi la collection d'objets que Sora conserve près de l'échelle menant à son lit, des poupées « Sonny Angel » de chez Dreams et une statuette d'Astro Boy en verre de chez Kiddy Land Tokyo.

P. 413 Daughters Sora and Umi have adjacent beds perched up above storage units. The structure is made from white Fin-Ply. • Unter den einander gegenüberliegenden Betten der Töchter Sora und Umi wurden verkleidete Stauräume integriert. Die Konstruktion besteht aus weißen Fin-Ply-Verschalungsplatten. • Les lits de Sora et d'Umi sont perchés au-dessus d'espaces de rangement. La structure est en Fin-Ply blanc.

ORNE
LOWER NORMANDY, FRANCE

OWNER An art collector **OCCUPATION** CEO
PROPERTY House, 450 sqm/4,850 sq ft gross floor; 3 floors; 4 rooms;
4 bathrooms **YEAR** Building: 1973, Remodelling: 2000 **ARCHITECT** Pierre Dreux
INTERIOR DESIGNER Emmanuel Renoird **PHOTOGRAPHER** Marco Tassinari/studiopep

A 1970s space-age house inspired by postwar futuristic American architecture. Original features like sculpted ceilings were maintained and a collection of contemporary art and "pop" design installed.
Ein Haus aus den 1970ern, das von futuristischer amerikanischer Nachkriegsarchitektur inspiriert ist. Ursprüngliche Konstruktionsmerkmale wie die skulptierten Decken blieben unverändert und wurden durch eine Sammlung aus zeitgenössischer Kunst und „Pop"-Design ergänzt.
Une maison « Space Age » des années 1970 inspirée de l'architecture futuriste américaine de l'après-guerre. Des détails originaux comme les plafonds sculptés ont été conservés et l'intérieur a été aménagé avec une collection d'art contemporain et de mobilier design « Pop ».

P. 414 An Osmany Laffita cow. • Eine Kuh von Osmany Laffita. • Une vache d'Osmany Laffita.

P. 415 An Arik Levy "Rock" table under the wavy living room ceiling. • Ein „Rock"-Tisch von Arik Levy unter der gewellten Wohnzimmerdecke. • Sous le plafond ondoyant du séjour, une table « Rock » d'Arik Levy.

← Saarinen's "Tulip" chairs surround an Italian dining table. • Saarinens „Tulip"-Stühle um den italienischen Esstisch. • Des chaises « Tulip » de Saarinen et une table de salle à manger italienne.

PP. 418–419 The "Bubble" lights in the master bedroom from Flos. • „Bubble"-Leuchten im Hauptschlafzimmer von Flos. • Dans la chambre principale, plafonniers « Bubble » de Flos.

← The violet bedroom features a stainless-steel wall sculpture. • Eine Edelstahlskulptur an der Wand des violetten Schlafzimmers. • Dans la chambre violette, une sculpture en inox.

↑ The oak ceiling has remained in place. • Die Eichendecke blieb unverändert. • Le plafond est d'origine.

PP. 422–423 The pool has a disco ball and black glass walls. • Discokugel und Glaswände im Schwimmbad. • La piscine avec une boule disco et des murs en verre noir.

PARATY

RIO DE JANEIRO, BRAZIL

OWNERS A young Brazilian couple **PROPERTY** House, 840 sqm/9,040 sq ft gross floor;
3 floors; 5 rooms; 9 bathrooms **YEAR** Building: 2009 **ARCHITECT** Marcio Kogan Studio MK27,
www.studiomk27.com.br **INTERIOR DESIGNERS** Marcio Kogan, Diana Radomysler & Carolina Castroviejo,
Studio MK27 **PHOTOGRAPHER** Matthieu Salvaing, www.matthieusalvaing.com

A summer house on the beach, accessible only by boat. It consists of two reinforced concrete boxes, one on top of the other, with a 27-metre (88.5 feet) span of glass windows and a stellar collection of Brazilian pop art and 20th-century design furniture.

Ein Sommerhaus am Strand. Es besteht aus zwei übereinandergebauten Kästen aus Stahlbeton und besticht durch eine 27 Meter lange Glasfront, eine herausragende Sammlung brasilianischer Pop-Art sowie durch Designermöbel aus dem 20. Jahrhundert.

Une maison de vacances sur une plage, qui est composée de deux boîtes superposées en béton armé et inclut une baie vitrée de 27 mètres de long. À l'intérieur, une superbe collection de Pop Art brésilien et de mobilier design du 20e siècle.

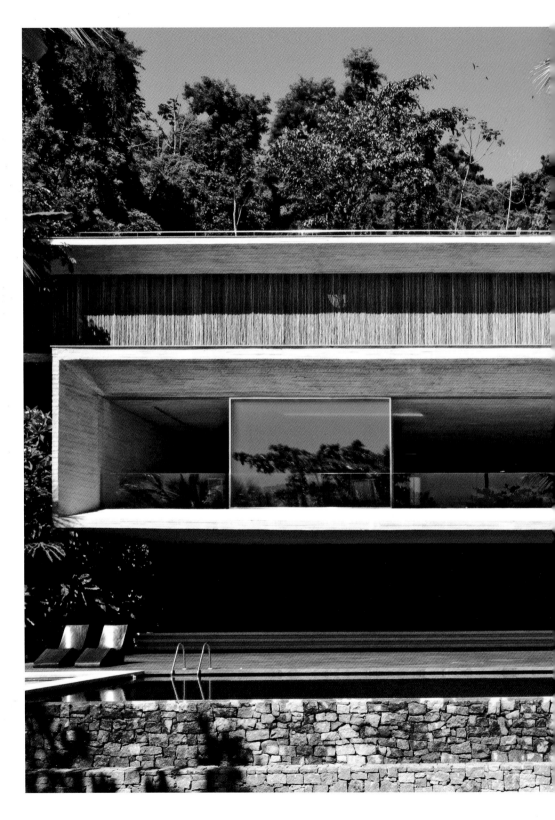

P. 424 The house projects from the mountain, surrounded by jungle. Its roof terraces act as viewing decks as well as a herb and sculpture garden. • Das Haus ist von Urwald umgeben. Das Dach wurde mit Terrassen versehen, die gleichzeitig als Aussichtsplattformen sowie als Kräuter- und Skulpturengarten dienen. • La maison est construite à flanc de montagne dans la jungle. Sur son toit, des terrasses panoramiques accueillent un jardin d'herbes aromatiques et un jardin de sculptures.

P. 425 Brightly coloured lounge chairs are lined up on the ipé wood deck by the pool. • Liegestühle in leuchtenden Farben, aufgereiht auf dem Deck aus Ipé-Holz am Pool. • Au bord de la piscine, des chaises longues vivement colorées alignées sur une terrasse en ipé.

PP. 426-427 Eucalyptus stick screens protect the upper floor bedrooms from the sun. • Blenden aus Eukalyptusholz schützen die Schlafzimmer im Obergeschoss vor der Sonne. • A l'étage

supérieur, un écran en tiges d'eucalyptus protège les chambres du soleil.

↑ Bisazza tiles in the shower. • Bisazza-Fliesen in der Dusche. • Carrelage de chez Bisazza.

→ A Nakashima armchair. • Ein Sessel von Nakashima. • Fauteuil de Nakashima.

← A José Zanine Caldas dining table and George Nakashima chairs. • Esstisch von José Zanine Caldas und Stühle von George Nakashima. • Table de José Zanine Caldas et chaises de George Nakashima.

→ The kitchen with a patio. • Küche mit Innenhof. • La cuisine et le patio.

PP. 432–433 The living room features furniture by Joaquin Tenreiro, Vladimir Kagan, and Gaetano Pesce. • Das Wohnzimmer mit Möbeln von Joaquin Tenreiro, Vladimir Kagan und Gaetano Pesce. • Dans le séjour, des meubles de Joaquin Tenreiro, Vladimir Kagan et Gaetano Pesce.

"I wanted to create a respectful contrast with the heavenly surroundings."

„Ich wollte einen respektvollen Kontrast zu der himmlischen Umgebung herstellen."
« J'ai voulu créer un contraste respectueux de l'environnement paradisiaque. »

PUNTA DEL ESTE
MALDONADO, URUGUAY

OWNERS Javier & Gerardo Gentile **OCCUPATION** Architects
PROPERTY Villa, 700 sqm/7,500 sq ft gross floor; 1 floor; 4 rooms; 3 bathrooms
YEAR Building: 2006 **ARCHITECTS** Javier & Gerardo Gentile,
Dealma, www.dealma.net **INTERIOR DESIGNERS** Javier Gentile & Juan Ricci
PHOTOGRAPHER Ricardo Labougle, www.ricardolabougle.com
PHOTO PRODUCER Ana Cardinale, www.anacardinale.com

In line with the local architectural vocabulary, wood, stone and cement were used. The interior was painted green: according to the principles of feng shui, this colour corresponds to the energetic core of the heart.
Für den Bau des Hauses wurden – wie in der Region üblich – Holz, Stein und Zement verwendet. Entsprechend den Prinzipien des Feng-Shui sind die Innenräume grün gestrichen: Die Farbe soll mit dem energetischen Zentrum des Herzens korrespondieren.
Conforme à l'architecture locale, la maison a été construite en bois, pierre et ciment. Les intérieurs ont été peints en vert selon les principes du feng shui. La couleur correspondrait au centre énergique du cœur.

P. 434 The stone around the pool comes from 100 km (60 miles) away. The custom daybeds are made from lapacho wood, while the two orange chairs date from the 1960s. • Die Steine für die Pool-Einfassung wurden 100 km entfernt abgebaut. Die Liegen sind Spezialanfertigungen aus Lapacho-Holz. Die beiden orangefarbenen Stühle stammen aus den 1960ern. • Les pierres autour de la piscine viennent d'un lieu situé à 100 km. Les lits de repos ont été réalisés spécialement pour la maison en lapacho. Les deux fauteuils orange datent des années 1960.

P. 435 The table in this outdoor porch was once part of Montevideo train station. The wire bird cages were purchased locally. • Der Tisch auf der Veranda gehörte einst zum Inventar des Bahnhofs von Montevideo. Die Vogelkäfige kaufte der Besitzer vor Ort. • Dans le porche ouvert, une table provenant de la gare ferroviaire de Montevideo. Les cages en fil de fer ont été achetées dans la région.

← The 1960s table contrasts with the laminate and stainless steel kitchen. • Der Tisch kontrastiert mit der Küche aus Schichtholz und Edelstahl. • Cette table des années 1960 contraste avec la cuisine en laminé et inox.

↑ The Bertoia-style chairs have leather seat pads. • Stühle im Stil von Bertoia mit Sitzpolstern aus Leder. • Les chaises inspirées de Bertoia sont tressées de cuir.

PP. 438–439 1960s armchairs, a red fibre-glass seat and Czech vases in the living room. • Im Wohnzimmer: Sessel aus den 1960ern, ein roter Glasfaser-Sessel und tschechische Vasen. • Dans le séjour, deux fauteuils des années 1960, un siège rouge en fibre de verre et des vases tchèques.

PP. 440–441 The 1960s chair in the master bedroom is American. The two standard lamps are from Flos. • Der Stuhl im Hauptschlafzimmer stammt aus den 1960ern. Die beiden Stehlampen sind von Flos. • Le fauteuil des années 1960 est américain. Deux lampadaires de chez Flos.

ROME
PIGNETO, ITALY

OWNERS Roberta Paolucci & Paolo Giacomelli **OCCUPATION** Jewellery designers
PROPERTY House, 150 sqm/1,600 sq ft gross floor; 1 floor;
4 rooms; 2 bathrooms **YEAR** Building: 1930s, Remodelling: 2004
PHOTOGRAPHER Alessandra Ianniello/studiopep

A 1930s farmhouse transformed by a modern extension. Open spaces were created by doing away with internal doors. The owners juxtaposed industrial materials with refined vintage pieces and modern design.
Ein Bauernhaus aus den 1930ern wurde durch einen modernen Anbau verwandelt. Im Inneren schuf man offene Räume. Die Besitzer kombinierten industrielle Materialien mit erlesenen klassischen Stücken und modernem Design.
Une ferme des années 1930 transformée. Les portes ont été ôtées pour créer des espaces ouverts. Les propriétaires ont juxtaposé des matériaux industriels à de beaux meubles anciens et modernes.

← Glass ceiling lights from the 1950s above the 19th-century dining table. • Gläserne Deckenleuchten aus den 1950ern hängen über einem Esstisch aus dem 19. Jahrhundert. • Des plafonniers en verre des années 1950 sont suspendus au-dessus d'une table de salle à manger du 19ᵉ siècle.

→ In the room of the owners' son, Rocco, is an old Italian school desk and a modular shelving system. • Ein italienisches Schulpult und ein Modulregal im Zimmer von Rocco, dem Sohn der Besitzer. • Dans la chambre de Rocco, le fils des propriétaires, un bureau d'écolier et un meuble de rangement modulaire.

P. 442 A view of the garden from the master bedroom. A cotton awning has been installed to provide shade for the ipé wood deck. The tub is made from slate and concrete. • Blick vom Hauptschlafzimmer in den Garten. Über dem Deck aus Ipé-Holz spenden Sonnensegel aus Baumwollstoff Schatten. Das Becken besteht aus Schiefer und Beton. • Une vue du jardin depuis la chambre principale. Des auvents en coton projettent une ombre bienvenue sur la terrasse en ipé. La baignoire est en ardoise et béton.

P. 443 The 1950s coffee table was found in a second-hand shop in Rome and the vintage Arne Jacobsen chair in a Turin street market. • Den Couchtisch aus den 1950ern entdeckten die Besitzer in einem Secondhand-Laden in Rom und den klassischen Stuhl von Arne Jacobsen auf einem Straßenmarkt in Turin. • La table basse des années 1950 a été dénichée dans un dépôt-vente à Rome et la chaise d'Arne Jacobsen dans un vide-grenier à Turin.

PP. 446–449 On the desk is a Pietro Bologna photographic print on silver sheet; the brick of the old farm building has been left exposed in the living room. • Auf dem Schreibtisch steht ein Fotodruck auf Silberblech von Pietro Bologna; die Ziegel wurden im Wohnzimmer sichtbar gelassen. • La photo sur le bureau est une épreuve argentique de Pietro Bologna ; dans le séjour, les briques ont été laissées apparentes.

"The house developed a hybrid identity,
with a distinctive inorganic sex appeal."

„Das Haus entwickelte eine hybride Identität mit
einem ausgeprägt unorganischen Sex-Appeal."
« La maison a développé une identité hybride et dégage
un sex-appeal non-organique très particulier. »

P. 450 In one corner of the master bedroom, a Nan Goldin photo hangs above a "Woodline" tub designed by Giampaolo Benedini for Agape. The office chair dates from the 1960s. • In einer Ecke des Hauptschlafzimmers hängt eine Fotografie von Nan Goldin über einer „Woodline"-Wanne, die Giampaolo Benedini für Agape entworfen hat. Der Bürostuhl ist aus den 1960ern. • Dans un coin de la chambre principale, une photo de Nan Goldin est accrochée au-dessus d'une baignoire « Woodline » conçue par Giampaolo Benedini pour Agape. La chaise de bureau date des années 1960.

P. 451 A late 19th-century chandelier hangs above the bed. The vintage Indian carpet is stitched with metallic thread. • Über dem Bett hängt ein Kronleuchter aus dem späten 19. Jahrhundert. Der klassische indische Teppich ist mit Metallfäden bestickt. • Un lustre de la fin du 19ᵉ siècle est suspendu au-dessus du lit. Le tapis indien ancien est cousu de fils d'argent.

← In the living room, a Buddha on metal sheet bought on Bali sits atop an early 20th-century filing cabinet, which the owners found in the house. • Im Wohnzimmer steht eine Blechtafel mit Buddha-Motiv aus Bali auf einem Aktenschrank

aus dem frühen 20. Jahrhundert, den die Besitzer im Haus fanden. • Dans le séjour, un bouddha imprimé sur une feuille métallique, acheté à Bali, trône sur un cartonnier du début du 20ᵉ siècle que les propriétaires ont trouvé dans la ferme.

↑ A crystal and brass Italian chandelier from the 1950s adds a touch of sparkle to the master bathroom. • Ein aus Kristall und Messing gefertigter italienischer Kronleuchter aus den 1950ern verleiht dem Hauptbadezimmer ein wenig Glamour. • Dans la chambre principale, un lustre italien des années 1950 en cristal et cuivre.

ROTTERDAM
SOUTH HOLLAND, NETHERLANDS

OWNERS Ghislaine van de Kamp & Sjoerd Didden **OCCUPATION** MA student &
Wigmaker for theatre and film **PROPERTY** House, 300 sqm/3,300 sq ft gross floor;
2 floors; 5 rooms; 3 bathrooms **YEAR** Building: 1918, Remodelling: 2007
ARCHITECTS & INTERIOR DESIGNERS Winy Maas, Jacob van Rijs & Nathalie de Vries/MVRDV,
www.mvrdv.nl **STRUCTURE** Pieters Bouwtechniek, Delft, www.pietersbouwtechniek.nl
CONTRACTOR Formaat Bouw, Sliedrecht **PHOTOGRAPHER** Stijn & Marie
PHOTO STYLIST Ben Zuydwijk

A daring extension on top of an old textile factory. The architects decided to make it stand out by coating it in bright blue polyurea. For the interiors, the owners also opted for a colourful, expressive style.
Eine ziemlich gewagte Aufstockung einer ehemaligen Textilfabrik. Die Architekten entschieden, dass sich der Bau von seiner Umgebung abheben sollte, und versahen ihn mit einer Beschichtung aus blauem Polyurea. Auch für die Innenräume wählten die Besitzer einen farbenfrohen, expressiven Stil.
Une audacieuse extension sur le toit d'une ancienne filature. Les architectes ont choisi de la faire se détacher de son environnement grâce à un revêtement polyuré bleu vif. A l'intérieur, les propriétaires ont également opté pour un style expressif et coloré.

P. 454 From the sky, it's impossible to miss MVRDV's roof extension to this private home. Three bedrooms were added, each in a distinctive house shape. • Aus der Luft ist MVRDVs Aufstockung nicht zu übersehen. Es wurden drei Schlafzimmer angebaut, jedes in der unverkennbaren Form eines frei stehenden Hauses. • Vu du ciel, on remarque l'agrandissement de la résidence réalisé par le cabinet MVRDV. Trois chambres ont été ajoutées, chacune ayant la forme d'une maisonnette.

P. 455 The blue polyurea coating was applied by Kunststof Coatings. For archi-

tect Winy Maas, the colour was chosen because "it connects [the building] to the sky." • Die Sprühbeschichtung aus blauem Polyurea wurde von Kunststof Coatings angebracht. Architekt Winy Maas wählte die Farbe, weil „sie [das Haus] mit dem Himmel verbindet". • Le revêtement polyuré bleu a été appliqué par Kunststof Coatings. Selon l'architecte Winy Maas, la couleur a été choisie parce qu'elle « relie [le bâtiment] au ciel ».

← The roof furniture got the same polyurea treatment as the rest of the structure. • Die Möbel auf der Terras-

se erhielten ebenfalls einen Polyurea-Überzug. • Sur la terrasse, les meubles ont été traités en bleu comme le reste de la structure.

↑ Red stools by Toon van Deijne. In the background, a Rody Graumans "85 Lamps" chandelier hangs above the dining table. • Die roten Hocker von Toon van Deijne. Im Hintergrund ein „85 Lamps"-Kronleuchter von Rody Graumans. • Les tabourets rouges sont de Toon van Deijne. A l'arrière-plan, un lustre « 85 Lamps » de Rody Graumans au-dessus de la table de salle à manger.

PP. 458–459   In the living room is a
Jasper Morrison sofa and a chair by Rob
Eckhardt. • Ein Sofa von Jasper Morrison,
ein Stuhl von Rob Eckhardt im Wohnzim-
mer. • Dans le séjour, un canapé de Jasper
Morrison et un fauteuil de Rob Eckhardt.

←   The staircases created by MVRDV
do not touch the floor. Instead, they are

suspended from a metal frame laid over
the original structure. • Die von MVRDV
gebaute Treppe berührt nicht den Boden:
Sie hängt an einem Metallrahmen, der
über die ursprüngliche Tragekonstruk-
tion gelegt wurde. • L'escalier créé
par MVRDV ne touche pas le sol mais
est suspendu dans un cadre métallique
superposé à la structure d'origine.

↑   The boys' rooms are accessed by
two staircases, which twine around
each other in a double helix form. •
Die Jungenzimmer sind über zwei
Treppen erreichbar, die sich in einer
Doppelhelix umeinanderschlingen. •
On accède aux chambres des garçons
par deux escaliers qui s'enroulent l'un
dans l'autre en double hélice.

SÃO PAULO

BRAZIL

OWNER A Brazilian art dealer **PROPERTY** House,
600 sqm/6,500 sq ft gross floor; 3 floors; 5 rooms; 4 bathrooms
YEAR Building: 1970, Remodelling: 2000 **ARCHITECT** Paulo Mendes da Rocha
PHOTOGRAPHER Andrea Ferrari, www.andreaferrari.info
PHOTO STYLIST Taissa Buescu

Built by Pritzker Prize winner Paulo Mendesda Rocha, this raw concrete house is a classic of Paulista Brutalist architecture. Light floods in through the roof, the interior is open, the minimal furnishings are very select.
Dieses Sichtbeton-Haus ist ein klassisches Beispiel für den Brutalismus der Paulista-Schule und wurde von dem Pritzker-Preisträger Paulo Mendes da Rocha gebaut. Das Innere ist sehr offen, und bei der Ausstattung beschränkte sich der Hausherr auf wenige Stücke.
Construite par Paulo Mendes da Rocha, lauréat du prix Priztker, cette maison en béton brut est un exemple classique de l'architecture brutaliste de São Paulo. Une lumière abondante tombe du toit, l'intérieur est ouvert et les meubles sont triés sur le volet.

P. 462 A Jarbas Lopes bicycle sculpture covered with natural-fibre vine stands behind a Flexform sofa in the living room. • Eine Fahrrad-Skulptur von Jarbas Lopes, verkleidet mit Naturfasern, steht hinter einem Flexform-Sofa im Wohnzimmer. • Dans le séjour, une sculpture bicyclette tapissée de fibres naturelles, œuvre de Jarbas Lopes, derrière un canapé de chez Flexform.

P. 463 Under the raw concrete staircase is a work by the Brazilian artist Marepe entitled "Acoustic Head." The painting of the tattooed woman is by Naoto Kawahara. • Unter der Sichtbeton-Treppe steht eine Arbeit des

brasilianischen Künstlers Marepe mit dem Titel „Acoustic Head". Das Gemälde der tätowierten Frau schuf Naoto Kawahara.• Sous l'escalier en béton brut, une œuvre de l'artiste brésilien Marepe intitulée « Acoustic Head ». Le tableau représentant la femme tatouée est de Naoto Kawahara.

↑ Behind the two Flávio de Carvalho chairs is a console on which works by Javier Velasco and Valeska Soares are presented. • Hinter den beiden Stühlen von Flávio de Carvalho steht eine Konsole, auf der Arbeiten von Javier Velasco und Valeska Soares präsentiert sind. • Derrière les deux fauteuils de Flávio de

Carvalho, des œuvres de Javier Velasco et de Valeska Soares sont exposées sur une console.

→ Two Frank Gehry "Hat Trick" chairs and a cardboard chair by the Brazilian group 100T are grouped around a burnt wood table created by the owner. • Zwei „Hat Trick"-Stühle von Frank Gehry und ein Pappkarton-Stuhl der brasilianischen Gruppe 100T sind um einen Tisch aus geflämmtem Holz gruppiert, den der Besitzer gebaut hat. • Deux fauteuils « Hat Trick » de Frank Gehry et un siège en carton du groupe brésilien 100T entourent une petite table en bois brûlé créée par le maître des lieux.

← The exquisitely sculptural curve of the stairs. • Die wunderbar geschwungene skulpturale Treppe. • La superbe courbe de l'escalier sculptural.

↑ A view of the living room from the floor above. • Blick vom oberen Geschoss ins Wohnzimmer. • Le séjour vu de l'étage supérieur.

← A Zhang Dali painting hangs by the bridge connecting the bedrooms. • Ein Gemälde von Zhang Dali neben der Brücke, die die Schlafzimmer verbindet. • Une peinture de Zhang Dali est accrochée près de la passerelle reliant les chambres.

↑ On the walls of the gallery leading to the bedrooms are works by Mari Eastman and Taro Shinoda, among others. • An den Wänden der Galerie, die zu den Schlafzimmern führt, hängen unter anderem Arbeiten von Mari Eastman und Taro Shinoda. • Sur les murs de la galerie menant aux chambres, des œuvres de Mari Eastman et Taro Shinoda entre autres.

PP. 470–471 "Spaghetti" chairs by Giandomenico Belotti at the dining table. The artwork in the background is by Lin Tianmiao. • „Spaghetti"-Stühle von Giandomenico Belotti am Esstisch. Im Hintergrund ein Werk von Lin Tianmiao. • Des chaises « Spaghetti » de Giandomenico Belotti entourent la table de salle à manger. Au mur, une œuvre de Lin Tianmiao.

SHANGHAI
LUWAN DISTRICT, CHINA

OWNER Richard Hsu **OCCUPATION** Design and brand consultant
PROPERTY Loft, 500 sqm/5,400 sq ft gross floor; 2 floors; 5 rooms; 3 bathrooms
YEAR Building: 1970s, Remodelling: 2007 **ARCHITECT &**
INTERIOR DESIGNER Richard Hsu, H+ Branding
PHOTOGRAPHER Reto Guntli/TASCHEN, www.retoguntli.com

On the top floor of a former hardware factory, this duplex offers great views, high ceilings and generous terraces. White walls form a backdrop for a mix of Eastern and Western, modern and old furnishings.

Diese Maisonette-Wohnung im obersten Stock einer ehemaligen Eisenwarenfabrik bietet eine fantastische Aussicht. Durch den Umbau entstanden loftartige Räume, und die weiß gestrichenen Wände bilden einen klaren Hintergrund für die östlichen und westlichen Möbel.

Perché au sommet d'une ancienne usine de quincaillerie, ce duplex dispose de vues superbes et de vastes terrasses. Ses espaces ont été peints en blanc pour offrir un écrin neutre à un mélange choisi de meubles occidentaux et orientaux, modernes et anciens.

P. 472 Hsu relaxes with his dogs Wolf and Duke on an outdoor terrace. The mattresses are upholstered with a thick washable cotton. • Hsu entspannt sich mit seinen Hunden Wolf und Duke auf der Dachterrasse. Die Matratzen sind mit einem dicken, waschbaren Baumwollstoff bezogen. • Hsu se détend avec ses chiens Wolf et Duke sur une des terrasses. Les matelas sont tapissés d'une épaisse toile en coton lavable.

P. 473 On the dining table are two statuettes of Mao and copies of ancient temple candle holders. The view takes in the neighbouring shikumen-style houses. • Auf dem Esstisch stehen zwei Statuetten von Mao und Kopien antiker Tempel-Kerzenleuchter. Im Hintergrund sieht man Häuser im Shikumen-Stil. • Sur la table de salle à manger, deux statuettes de Mao et des copies de bougeoirs de temple anciens. La vue donne sur des shikumen, des maisons typiques de Shanghai.

PP. 474–475 Hsu designed the dining table based on an old Chinese scholar's table. The antique chairs come from China, Thailand, Malaysia and Singapore. • Hsu ließ sich beim Entwurf für den Esstisch von einem antiken chinesischen Tisch eines Gelehrten inspirieren. Rechts antike Stühle aus China, Thailand, Malaysia und Singapur. • Hsu a dessiné la table de salle à manger d'après une ancienne table d'étude chinoise. Sur la droite, une collection de chaises anciennes provenant de Chine, de Thaïlande, de Malaisie et de Singapour.

↑ Visitors often write and draw on the blackboard, which separates the living area from the conference room. Hsu designed the sofa himself. • Besucher schreiben und malen oft etwas auf die Tafel, die den Wohnbereich vom Konferenzraum trennt. Das Sofa ist ein Eigenentwurf von Hsu. • Le tableau noir qui sépare la salle de conférence du séjour sert souvent aux visiteurs pour laisser un message ou un dessin. Hsu a dessiné lui-même le canapé.

↑ The bathroom is located in a glass-house-like structure on the upper floor. • Das Badezimmer ist in einer treibhaus-artigen Konstruktion im Obergeschoss untergebracht. • La salle de bain est située dans une structure en verre à l'étage supérieur.

→ The bamboo ladder has travelled with Hsu for many years. It's often been used as a towel rack. • Die Bambusleiter reist seit vielen Jahren mit Hsu und wird oft als Handtuchhalter genutzt. • L'échelle en bambou accompagne Hsu depuis de longues années. Elle a souvent servi de porte-serviettes.

P. 477 The cantilevered timber steps lead to the bedroom and bathroom. • Die Holztreppe führt zu Schlafzimmer und Bad. • Les marches en bois mènent à la chambre et la salle de bain.

PP. 480–481 In the open kitchen, custom stools are grouped around a mah-jong table. What looks like a wicker seat to the left is actually a light bought in Thailand. • In der offenen Küche sind maßgefertigte Hocker um einen Mah-jong-Tisch gruppiert. Was aussieht wie

ein Korbsessel, ist eine in Thailand gekaufte Leuchte. • Dans la cuisine ouverte, des tabourets réalisés sur mesure sont regroupés autour d'une table de mah-jong. Sur la gauche, ce qui ressemble à un siège est en fait une lampe achetée en Thaïlande.

TRANCOSO

BAHIA, BRAZIL

OWNER Wilbert Das **OCCUPATION** Designer
PROPERTY House, 192 sqm/2,070 sq ft gross floor; 1 floor;
4 rooms; 4 bathrooms **YEAR** Remodelling: 2010
INTERIOR DESIGNER Wilbert Das, www.wilbertdas.com **PHOTOGRAPHER &**
PHOTO PRODUCER Mirjam Bleeker, www.mirjambleeker.nl

Situated on the main square, the property consists of three houses. "I have always preferred to restore historical buildings by paying homage to their history and materials," says Das. He painted the insides white and removed walls to create loft-like spaces.

Das Anwesen besteht aus drei Häusern. „Ich habe schon immer lieber historische Gebäude restauriert und dabei ihrer Geschichte und ihren Materialien Ehrerbietung erwiesen", so Das. Er ließ die Innenräume weiß streichen und einige Wände entfernen.

Cette propriété est composée de trois maisons. Wilbert Das explique : « J'ai toujours préféré restaurer des bâtiments historiques en rendant hommage à leur histoire et à leurs matériaux. » A l'intérieur, espaces ouverts et murs blancs.

P. 482 The property is named after a former inhabitant Irenio, known locally as "the magician." • Das Anwesen ist nach dem früheren Besitzer Irenio benannt, der im Ort als „der Zauberer" bekannt war. • La propriété porte le nom de l'un de ses anciens occupants, Irenio, connu ici comme « le magicien ».

P. 483 Das created the banquette base using recycled construction wood. Three of the pillows have been made with Brazilian coffee bean bags. • Das baute eine Bank aus recyceltem Bauholz. Drei der Kissen wurden aus brasilianischen Kaffeesäcken genäht. • Das a créé le socle de la banquette avec du bois de construction recyclé. Trois des coussins ont été réalisés avec d'anciens sacs utili-

sés pour le transport des grains de café brésiliens.

PP. 484–485 A hammock hangs outside one of the buildings. • Eine Hängematte vor einem der Häuser. • Un hamac suspendu devant l'un des bâtiments.

↑ The property consists of three buildings surrounded by a 1,000 sqm (10,800 sq ft) garden planted with numerous fruit trees. • Das Anwesen besteht aus drei Häusern, umgeben von einem 1000 qm großen Garten, der mit zahlreichen Obstbäumen bepflanzt ist. • La propriété compte trois bâtiments entourés d'un jardin de 1000 m² planté de nombreux arbres fruitiers.

→ View towards a bedroom suite. • Blick auf ein Schlafzimmer. • Une vue de l'une des chambres.

PP. 488–489 The sofa was designed by Das and made by a local carpenter. The painted terracotta vase comes from a local ceramic studio. • Das Sofa wurde von Das entworfen und von einem lokalen Schreiner gebaut. Die bemalte Terrakottavase kommt aus einer Keramikwerkstatt im Ort. • Le canapé a été dessiné par Das et réalisé par un menuisier de la région. Le vase en terre cuite peint vient d'un atelier de céramique local.

P. 490 Das was particularly attracted by the simplicity. The shutters are original to the house. The open brick cupboard is original to the house. It has been painted white and illuminated by sunlight through glass roof tiles. • Das belieẞ die Fensterläden in ihrem Originalzustand. Das gemauerte Regal stammt noch aus dem ursprünglichen Gebäude. Es wurde weiẞ gestrichen und erhält durch Glasdachziegel Tageslicht von oben. • Das a été séduit par la simplicité des lieux. Les volets sont d'origine. Le dressoir en briques se trouvait déjà dans la maison. Repeint en blanc, il est mis en valeur par la lumière naturelle qui filtre par les tuiles en verre du toit.

P. 491 The dining area screen is the frame of the old clay wall. The table was made locally using recycled wood. • Der Wandschirm vor dem Essbereich besteht aus dem Gerüst der Lehmwand. Der Tisch wurde vor Ort aus recyceltem Holz gefertigt. • Dans la salle à manger, le paravent est la structure de l'ancienne cloison en terre battue. La table a été réalisée avec du bois recyclé.

↑ Aquamarine was chosen for the shutters of this guestroom to contrast with the red flowers outside. • Bei den Fensterläden dieses Gästezimmers entschied Das sich für Aquamarin, um einen Kontrast zu den roten Blumen der

Umgebung zu schaffen. • Dans cette chambre d'amis, les volets ont été peints en bleu-vert pour contraster avec les fleurs rouges à l'extérieur.

→ A view from one guestroom to another. The straw mat on the floor was made locally. • Blick durch die Gästezimmer. Die Strohmatte auf dem Boden wurde in der Region gefertigt. • Deux chambres d'amis en enfilade. Le tapis en paille est de l'artisanat local.

ZUOZ
GRAUBÜNDEN, SWITZERLAND

OWNER Monica De Cardenas **OCCUPATION** Art dealer
PROPERTY House, 500 sqm/5,400 sq ft gross floor; 3 floors; 10 rooms;
3 bathrooms **YEAR** Building: c. 1400, Remodelling: 2006
ARCHITECT & INTERIOR DESIGNER Hans-Jörg Ruch, www.ruch-arch.ch
PHOTOGRAPHER Filippo Bamberghi/OWI

A gallery in a 15th-century Engadin house. According to Monica De Cardenas, "the powerful presence of 600-year-old wooden ceilings and almost one-metre-thick (more than three-feet-thick) walls creates an ideal environment for contemporary art."

Eine Galerie in einem Haus aus dem 15. Jahrhundert im Engadin. Laut Besitzerin Monica De Cardenas „schafften die 600 Jahre alten Holzdecken und die fast ein Meter dicken Mauern den idealen Rahmen für Kunst".

Une galerie logée dans une maison du 15ᵉ siècle. Pour Monica De Cardenas, « la puissante présence des plafonds en bois vieux de 600 ans et des murs de près d'un mètre d'épaisseur crée un environnement idéal pour l'art contemporain ».

← The ladder leads up to a desk on the roof of the master bedroom. • Die Leiter führt hinauf zu einem Schreibtisch auf dem Dach des Hauptschlafzimmers. • L'échelle mène à un bureau installé sur le toit de la chambre principale.

→ In the office, an oil painting by Gianluca Di Pasquale hangs above an Engadin table dating from 1600. Tommaso Cimini designed the standard lamp for Lumina. • Im Büro hängt ein Gemälde von Gianluca Di Pasquale. Die Stehlampe ist ein Entwurf von Tommaso Cimini für Lumina. • Dans le bureau, une huile de Gianluca Di Pasquale au-dessus d'une table de l'Engadine datant de 1600. Le lampadairea été dessiné par Tommaso Cimini pour Lumina.

P. 494 Called "Chesa Albertini," the house is located in the beautiful village of Zuoz near St. Moritz. Like its neighbours, it has cowsheds and a barn. • Das „Chesa Albertini" genannte Haus liegt im schönen Dorf Zuoz in der Nähe von St. Moritz. Wie bei seinen Nachbarn gehören ein Kuhstall und eine Scheune zum Anwesen. • Baptisée «

Chesa Albertini », la maison est située dans le beau village de Zuoz près de St. Moritz. Comme ses voisines, elle possède une étable et une grange.

P. 495 In the dining room, a work by Christine Streuli hangs above a one-off sideboard created by Marion Klein. The door leads to the entrance. •

Im Esszimmer hängt eine Arbeit von Christine Streuli über einem Sideboard, einer Einzelanfertigung von Marion Klein. Die Tür im Hintergrund führt zum Eingang. • Dans la salle à manger, une œuvre de Christine Streuli est accrochée au-dessus de l'exemplaire unique d'un buffet conçu par Marion Klein. La porte donne sur l'entrée.

"A place for contemplation and thoughtfulness."

„Ein Ort der Kontemplation und der Bedächtigkeit."
« C'est un lieu propice à la contemplation et la réflexion. »

PP. 498–499 The wooden ceilings in the entrance hall are original to the house. • Die Holzdecken im Eingangsbereich des Hauses blieben unverändert. • Les plafonds en bois du hall d'entrée sont d'origine.

→ Tradition meets hi-tech. An old Engadin table and stools are juxtaposed with a stainless-steel kitchen from Strato. • Tradition trifft auf Hightech: ein alter Engadiner Tisch und Hocker neben einer Edelstahlküche von Strato. • Le mariage de la tradition et du high-tech. Une table et des chaises anciennes de l'Engadine côtoient une cuisine en inox de chez Strato.

PP. 502–503 A Christine Streuli work provides a splash of colour to a guestroom. • Im Gästezimmer sorgt eine Arbeit von Christine Streuli für Farbe. • Dans la chambre d'amis, une œuvre colorée de Christine Streuli.

IMPRINT

EACH AND EVERY TASCHEN BOOK PLANTS A SEED!

TASCHEN is a carbon neutral publisher. Each year, we offset our annual carbon emissions with carbon credits at the Instituto Terra, a reforestation program in Minas Gerais, Brazil, founded by Lélia and Sebastião Salgado. To find out more about this ecological partnership, please check: www.taschen.com/zerocarbon
Inspiration: unlimited. Carbon footprint: zero.

To stay informed about TASCHEN and our upcoming titles, please subscribe to our free magazine at www.taschen.com/magazine, follow us on Instagram and Facebook, or e-mail your questions to contact@taschen.com

Texts
Ian Phillips, Paris

French Translation
Philippe Safavi, Paris

German Translation
Franca Fritz & Heinrich Koop, Straelen

© 2022 TASCHEN GmbH
Hohenzollernring 53, D-50672 Köln
www.taschen.com

Original Edition
© 2011 TASCHEN GmbH

Printed in Bosnia-Herzegovina
ISBN 978-3-8365-9195-9

Page 2 Susanne & Matteo Thun, Capri, Italy
Photo: Hiepler & Brunier, www.hiepler-brunier.de
The walls of the main kitchen are covered with playful patchworks of tiles from L'Antica Ceramica.

Page 6 Paraty, Brazil
Photo: Matthieu Salvaing, www.matthieusalvaing.com
Brightly coloured lounge chairs are lined up on the ipé wood deck by the pool.

Page 9 Laurence Rigaill & Cyril Jean, Avignon, France
Photo: Marco Tassinari, www.marcotassinari.com
An Eero Aarnio "Ball Chair" stands on a round carpet. The dining table and chairs are from Eero Saarinen's iconic "Tulip" series.

Page 10 Orne, France
Photo: Marco Tassinari/studiopep
Stretched over three levels, the reinforced concrete structure looks out over an undulating park, measuring more than 35 acres.